© Phil M Jones 2012 All rights reserved

Published by Philmjones Ltd
Deco House,
170 Plymouth Road,
B97 4PA
United Kingdom

All rights reserved. No part of this publication may be reproduced, stored in retrieval system or transmitted in any form or by any means, electronic, mechanical, photocopying, recording or otherwise without the prior permission of the publisher.

While the publisher has taken reasonable care in the preparation of this book, the publisher makes no representation, express or implied, with regard to the accuracy of the information contained in this book and cannot accept legal responsibility or liability for any errors or omissions from the book or the consequences thereof.

Products or services that are referred to in this book may be either trademarks and/or registered trademarks of their respective owners. The publishers and author make no claims to these trademarks.

A CIP Catalogue record for this book is available from the British Library.

The moral rights of the author have been asserted.

Design by www.ebook-designs.co.uk

Printed in Great Britain by Lulu

ISBN - 978-1-4710-8724-0

TOOLBOX

Essential selling skills to
WIN MORE BUSINESS

PHIL M JONES

*For Mum, Dad,
Steph, Amelia
and Emily xx*

Preface

My journey in business started at a very young age and by starting young I started learning some important lessons very quickly.

Like all 14 year olds, I had big dreams and wanted all the finer things in life; including big stereos, the latest games consoles and all the games, the newest trainers, a celeb style wardrobe and the latest Sony Walkman. However the difference was that I was prepared to do something about it and not wait around for hand outs.

I initially gained a huge lesson from my father - my dad runs a small local building company and his biggest challenge was finding a reliable workforce. As such, me and my big mouth, offered to go to work with him for the reward of £20 a day. I swept up, tidied tools, cleared away rubbish, mixed cement, made teas and above all else was incredibly considerate of the environment I was working in. By the 3rd or 4th day of working my daily wage had tripled and I received a number of additional tips from customers. The lesson I had learnt was that of value. You get paid for what you do, not what you say you can do.

Seeing the world of business as a teenager is fantastic. You are free from experience and therefore full of confidence because you don't know what you don't know. What I did know was that I wanted more, so I set about thinking of things I could do to generate more cash. I wanted something regular, where people would keep coming back and that needed little or no money to get started. I had an idea. I picked up my wallet and visited Halfords to make my investment in my very first business. I bought a bucket, sponge, chamois leather and some car shampoo. I filled my bucket with enthusiasm and set to work, completely unaware of 3 of the biggest lessons I was about to learn.

Knocking on the first door, I had a set of words ready. "Excuse me, I am really sorry to bother you, but would you be interested in having your car washed?" People would answer with one of a number of responses: "No Thank you", "Can you come back next week?", "Yes please" were all common, however the most popular response was always "How much?", which I very quickly realised meant "I am interested". The main lesson here was: If you don't ask, then you don't get.

Understanding pricing soon followed. I started charging £3 a car and everyone was happy, so I went to £4 and nobody complained at all. It was in the pricing strategies that follow that taught more powerful lessons. I put the price up to £4.50 and everybody started giving me a fiver! A huge increase in profits for a marginal increase in price. Only in raising the price past £5 did I realise that I had hit my ceiling, as over £5 people stopped saying "yes". When was the last time you visited your pricing?

Business was buoyant for a teenager and I was soon in a position where my income was well in excess of all my fellow students and even exceeding a number of teachers! However, with no mobile phone, no advertising and no inbound enquiries I was a little concerned about staying in control of my customers. So, what I did was, after every car wash, I simply asked them when they would like it washed again. Booking the next transaction kept me in control and ensured that I maximised the number of opportunities from each customer.

By my 15th birthday I was doing okay - I had all the toys a teenager could imagine, most of the money saved for my first car, and was planning my first holiday without the parents.

So why share this with you? I have been learning all my life and have added to these lessons through a challenging and rewarding career; fortunately I have been keeping a record of these lessons as I go. These lessons now serve as my tools and this book is my chance to share these tools with you, so you can learn from my experiences and enjoy heightened success for yourself.

Contents

Introduction	**19**
Getting started	**21**
Two types of selling	23
Defining your target market	24
Building your prospect list	25
Essential Kit	27
Sales is a philosophy and not a department	29
Books are judged by their covers	31
Doing the right thing	35
Knowing your numbers	37
Confidence	**39**
People buy people	39
Levels of Success	40
It is tough	44
Making your own luck	46
Your competition	48
Opening doors	**51**
10-5-2	51
Networking for success	54
Questions for a room full of strangers	57
What face are you wearing?	57
Who is the most important person?	59

Contents	Toolbox
What's in a name?	61
Making yourself more memorable	64
Treat them as your best customer	64
My secret weapon	65
The phone call	68
Social Media 3 step plan	68
Magic Words – You couldn't do me a favour	72
Social Proof	73
A simple script for asking for testimonials	76
Another referral generation tool	76
Fishing in the same pond	77
Magic Words – If ..... Then	80
Become the expert	82
Bin the brochure	84
Winning Appointments	**85**
Just pick up the phone	85
Don't make cold calls	86
Two versions of yes	90
Be precious with your time	91
Be easy to contact	92
Visit the neighbours	93
How to guarantee an appointment	94
Winning the first sale	**97**
Who holds the controls?	97
Easy first "Yes"	101
Make it easy to buy	102
Magic Words – Most people	103

philmjones.com

Winning language	104
Put a bow on it	105
Your sales presentation	108
Magic Words – Just Imagine	111
Building Value – Presenting Price	112
Being Assumptive	114
Closing sentences that work	115
Dealing with faffers	116
Too much of a good thing	117
Have a down-sell	119
Buying triggers	120
Maximising opportunities	**121**
What are you leaving on the table?	121
Magic words – Enough	123
Prod the bruise	124
Peeling back the layers	126
2 ears and 1 mouth	127
What is this costing you?	128
The simple upsell	129
Product placement	131
Multi-buy offers	133
Membership	134
Asking for referrals	134
Data Capture	137
Feedback Forms	137
Be convenient	139
Waterproofing	139
Review old diaries and journals	142

| Contents | Toolbox |

Developing a team — **145**
- The art of sales management — 145
- You never get a second chance to make a first impression — 146
- Creatures of Habit — 146
- Give them a fine reputation to live up to — 147
- Manage results but measure activity — 149
- Let me show you — 150
- Be good enough to teach — 151

Dealing with indecision — **155**
- Avoiding objections — 155
- Magic words – I bet you are a bit like me…? — 158
- Overcoming Objections — 159
- Magic words – Just out of curiosity — 161
- Negotiate like a pro — 162
- The Big Negotiation — 165
- Magic Words – Don't Worry — 166
- Can I have a discount? — 167
- The conditional close — 169
- Be persistent — 170
- Playing Devil's Advocate — 172

Account Management — **175**
- The Database — 175
- The Drop in — 176
- The Courtesy call — 177
- The Newsletter — 177
- The E-newsletter — 178

Toolbox	Contents
The Blog	178
The Facebook page	179
The Twitter account	179
The Linkedin account	180
The Website	181
The Get together	182
The Letter	182
The Email offer	183
The Direct mail offer	185
The Gift	186
The Pat on the back	187
The text message	190
They all tune into the same station	190
It is the thought that counts	191
Acknowledgments	**195**
About the author	**197**

Introduction

I have attended countless seminars, read hundreds of books and invested time to learn from myriad exceptional people. However, the common denominator from all these activities is that I never took everything in. It is often said that 90% of everything you learn in a day is forgotten by the very next day.

When I decided to write this book I wanted to provide you with something that would serve you in many ways. I wanted you to be able read it cover to cover and be engaged and encouraged to take ideas and actions from it. I have also planned that you can use it as a resource for your own meetings and training sessions and, additionally, I wanted you to just be able to dip in and out of it during those quiet moments.

Not all of the ideas and principles are born from my mind. Many I have collected from years of time and money investment in myself. However, all that I share I have experienced; this is my take on what it takes to succeed in sales from years of practicing this essential art form.

This is without a doubt a working document so please highlight key points, take notes in this book and most importantly take action on the ideas you generate from it. I hope it lives up to my goals and in turn helps you achieve yours.

Chapter 1
Getting started

Finding yourself in a sales role is quite often an accident. Perhaps you have just started in business, had an urgent business need or maybe somebody else has put you into the role. The truth is - we are all sales people and in every part of life, sales skills are useful tools in helping us to reach the levels of success we are capable of.

Often the first hurdle in succeeding in sales is admitting to yourself that you are personally responsible to achieving success in sales and that 'sales' is not a dirty word. Very few children grow up aspiring to be in sales, yet countless top achievers in all areas of life had to be great sales people before they could be great at what they do.

I thought I would compile a list of famous sales professionals and see if you get my point.

- Tony Blair
- Katie Price
- Mohamed Ali

- Martin Luther King
- Nelson Mandella
- Sir Alex Ferguson
- Jamie Oliver
- Richard Branson
- Oprah Winfrey
- JK Rowling

You are probably feeling that there is a huge difference between your initial belief of the sales person and these decorated professionals. To explore this further I recently compiled a short survey to consider the perception of the world on both sales people and sales professionals and here are the results.

Sales People	Sales Professionals
Pushy	Good Listeners
Cocky	Understanding
Just after money	Friendly
Conman	Empathetic
Over-Friendly	Helpful
Liars	Genuine
Annoying	Knowledgeable

I found this really interesting and it is fair to say that if you are looking to be one of those in the left hand column then this book is probably not for you.

I would also go as far to say that if you ever receive the comment "you are a good salesman/women" then that is by no means a compliment and means that you have been caught selling.

What we are looking to do is to ethically grow our business and be recognised by our existing and potential customers with the descriptions from the right hand column. If that is the case then let's take a look at the steps to take to make this happen.

Two types of selling

Selling can be split into two camps. One camp is the "wait for it to happen" camp and the other is the "make it happen" camp.

Waiting for it to happen. This reactive approach relies on waiting for the phone to ring or customers to visit to make enquiries. You are then left to do the very best you can with the opportunities you are presented with. It is a lottery that big businesses with deep pockets and robust advertising campaigns have made work but is risky for smaller businesses.

Making it happen. The sales process and success in sales is all about maintaining control. If you wish to control your success you can take a proactive approach and take fate into your own hands. If you can succeed in this type of selling you can always prosper and gain the reactive business too. Relying purely on a reactive approach will bring huge variance with external factors largely responsible for your success.

Defining your target market

If you are looking for more customers then you must first choose what qualities are important in your ideal client. It amazes me that in all the speeches and seminars that I conduct, typically less than 25% of an audience have a clearly identified dream customer.

I would suggest that you approach this task in two ways. Firstly consider, in an ideal world, exactly who your dream customer would be. Think of Utopia and then take a reality check and write down the name of the person or individual who is your dream customer. Once you have got that name, write yourself a comprehensive list of all the reasons why that organisation would be your ideal customer.

Having this list of qualities is essential in framing your target market and is a fundamental building block when planning to grow your business. In addition to this list you may then wish to ask yourself the following questions about your target customers.

> - Where are they located?
> - How big are they?
> - Who is the decision maker?
> - Why would they need you?

Combining the answers to these questions with the qualities from your list will put you in a very strong position to firstly, identify your target customer and secondly, create a written profile describing exactly who you are looking for. Once you have that profile be sure to share it with all that you can.

If you have a range of products and services and have different target markets for each then simply repeat the process for each specific audience.

Building your prospect list

When proactively growing your business you will never have more new customers than you have prospects. Therefore an essential part of every sales process is to identify a list of potential customers and continually add to that list as often as possible. A never-ending prospect list is a vital tool in professional sales, however, the trouble is that it is often our responsibility to both fill it and convert it.

My general rule is to build a list with at least ten times more than the number of new customers you desire. Throughout the years I have devised a simple system to build a list of potential customers; you simply follow the FRIENDS system.

Friends - Start your list by considering all your friends in life and business. Go through your mobile phone, email contacts and address books and consider all people who fit your target market, or could help you get closer to your target market and then add them to your list.

Records - As we go through our professional lives we collect reams of information that is full of potential future value. Go through existing and previous customer and supplier records, contacts from previous employment and libraries of business cards.

Industry - Consider every industry that you would like to work with, or have worked with in the past, and then add relevant individuals and companies from the same or similar industries.

E-marketing - The web is a fantastic tool for building your list. Have a contact form on your website to collect phone and email addresses in exchange for something

Toolbox | Getting Started

of value, and use the social networks to identify existing buyers of your product and service

Networking – Attend events, both formal and informal, to identify future customers for you and your business

Directory – Utilise directories of groups and organisations within your sector to gain names and contact details of prospects. Start with the directories of groups you are associated to, so that you have a common interest to make contact over.

Same Name – Finally review your entire list and consider anyone that you can think of that shares the same Christian name or Surname to any of your existing prospects, you will be amazed at how many names you add by following this simple memory technique

Please remember that people buy people and that your list must be of names of people and not names of organisations!

Essential Kit

Going out into the market place is often a daunting experience which often results in people either being massively underprepared or hiding behind their

Getting Started — Toolbox

marketing literature. In every sales role I have impacted on there are some essential 'must haves' that are necessary to succeed. Everything else is just 'nice to have' or worse still, can stop you selling.

Notepad and Pen - Taking notes before, during and after meetings is a valuable commodity. It can ensure that you cover all you wish to cover, show that you are serious about doing business, help you listen effectively and ensure that all relevant agreements are actioned. Don't leave home without them.

Watch - Time is an incredibly valuable resource to both sales professionals and customers. Ensuring you respect it is paramount in your success. Wearing a watch is a visual indicator that you value time.

Diary – Without a diary you can't plan follow ups, re-schedule appointments or prioritise actions. Have it with you at all times.

A phone – The world of sales is fast paced and full of changing circumstances. The ability to communicate immediately is a necessity.

Accurate Client Records - From the beginning you should keep accurate records on all of your existing and potential customers. Whether it is a computer based CRM or a paper based set of client files, maintaining a fluid record of communications and information will win you masses of extra business.

Business Cards – Perhaps the most important individual piece of marketing literature you own. Make sure it represents you well, has all your contact information on it and that you have them available at all times. You never know when an opportunity may arise.

Order Forms – It may sound obvious but the number of times I have seen sales staff miss opportunities because they did not have the ability to take an order there and then…!

Many of you reading this are perhaps thinking that there is rakes of other kit that is essential in your business and perhaps you are right. However please consider that the sales person's job is to give the prospect enough information to make a decision and then ask for that decision.

Very often pre-prescribed sales presenters, product catalogues and samples can all give customers the feeling of being sold to and gain a response of indecision such as "Leave me a brochure and I will get back to you…"

Sales is a philosophy and not a department

In every business I have ever been a part of there has typically been a clear divide between the sales and the operational sides of the organisation. Most people believe that the responsibility of winning and maintaining business is simply that of the sales team. I do not just disagree with this approach, but believe it to be the failing of many businesses year after year.

If you are building a business that looks to connect with its customers, offer fantastic levels of service, get referrals from its customers and stacks of repeat business, then understanding that sales is a philosophy can really help you get there.

This fact was greatly reinforced to me during my time with Britain's leading furniture retailer, DFS. My time with DFS served as my apprenticeship to underpin the true power of adopting sales processes through every area of an organisation. Once this is achieved you can sit back and admire the success it creates.

Getting this right brings such significant results it's astounding. This very principle was the key factor in increasing turnover by millions of pounds and all by not having any more people through the door. This may sound great when applied to a large multi-national retailer but how can this apply to your business?

Having everybody pulling together in one direction creates benefits that are so slight when looked at in isolation, yet, the collective benefit is compounded to a result that can be astounding.

- Increase in revenue
- Increase in profits
- No late payments
- No bad debts
- Preferential treatment from suppliers
- Increased operational efficiency
- Improved staff productivity
- More free time
- Reduced customer complaints
- Improved communication

These are just a few benefits I have enjoyed from adopting these principles. Consider everyone in your business and ask yourself what effect they have on the sales process and how could they improve it? Then look at those who act operationally in your business, consider what challenges they are faced with and think how equipping them with some new skills will help them with that process.

Books are judged by their covers

Unfortunately, in life and business, first impressions count. As a race we are notoriously shallow and make judgements on others in the shortest periods of time and with very limited information.

However in the world of sales and with 'my glass is half full' approach I want to view this as an opportunity. What this means is that if we create the wrong first impression that it is all our fault, yet if we create the right first impression that is all our fault also. What I am trying to say is that this factor is within our complete control.

The position you hold in your business and the size and credibility of your organisation are all unknown factors when you present yourself for the first time. You really can make your own luck by pitching this at the appropriate level.

Your personal presentation is paramount. Your choice of outfit, fragrance, personal grooming, and accessories all say something about you. Are you happy with the message you are giving?

I am sure you can think of countless scenarios that you have been pre-judged or you have pre-judged others.

Toolbox   Getting Started

It is important to accept that this happens, but equally important to never pre-judge others.

The beauty of knowing we will be pre-judged is that we can do all we can to get this first impression right and I encourage you to consider the following:

Mode of transport – Peoples social standing is often judged on the car that they drive. Knowing this, please do all you can to use it as a tool. If your business requires you to be perceived as highly successful and your car echoes this then make sure you get seen driving it. If your vehicle hasn't yet reached your business aspirations, then choose an alternative means of transport, or ensure that it does not hinder your chances of success.

This works the other way too. If your business has a high value offering and your car seems too successful then you will be perceived as too expensive and may lose the work. What is imperative is that whatever your means of transport it is always presented at its best and is working for you and not against you.

Your uniform - Clothing is a tough one to get right. For many of us we undertake a variety of roles in business and have a very varied work life. My general rule is to dress as your customer would expect to see you and if in doubt you are better to be too smart than too casual.

Your accessories - Accessories are often the truest of tests to people's personalities. You can tell far more about people from their choice of shoes, jewellery, body art and luggage than any other factor. Please take a moment to consider what yours say about you and if they give off the impression you are planning for.

Your grooming – Be prepared for people to judge you by what you look like, what you smell like and how you behave. Ask a stranger to profile you based on your look and listen to the response. I learnt an important lesson on a hot summer's day, with a busy schedule and an important client meeting in the evening, to always have a change of clothes to hand. Without this change of clothes and access to shower facilities I am certain that I would have given the wrong first impression. Please also consider your handshake; too firm and people will think you're arrogant, too weak and they will think you are incompetent.

Your marketing materials - Your business gives off an impression too. Whether it is your business card, your e-mail signature, your telephone voicemail, or your website, that your prospects first bump into, be certain it is giving the right message. I work on the principle of presenting your business as the one you plan to grow into, not the one you are today. The quality of printing on your media gives an impression to the care and attention you take with your business. Giving a consistent message through all e-mail communication demonstrates structure and control and I would recommend that all e-mail communication follows the same format with fonts, spacing and auto-signatures all being consistent. Your voicemail sets the tone and culture of your business, your website should clearly explain how you help people and re- enforce your vision.

In my experience, every business that has gone to this extent to understand their personal and business brand has developed to within spitting distance of that vision.

Doing the right thing

What I soon learnt was that there is a big difference between doing the job right and doing the right job. I have always been hardworking, dedicated and put effort into every activity, striving towards the best results. The changing point came when I realised that just by working hard and being good at what I did only resulted in limited success. The big lesson was that I needed to understand what my high pay-off activities really are.

We all have "stuff" that we need to do in our daily routines but how much of that "stuff" really helps towards achieving the end result we are looking for. Run this simple equation for yourself.

You will need to know the answers to the following questions.

A) How much money do you wish to earn in the next 12 months?
B) How many hours a week do you plan to work personally?
C) How many weeks a year do you see yourself working?

Then calculate the following mathematical equation.

A ÷ B ÷ C = Your hourly rate

Only in knowing this number could I really start to look at my productivity and all the things that I was doing that did not help me to build a business. Anything that I was doing that I would not pay myself my desired hourly rate to do, I had to come up with an alternative.

Many of the activities you may have to learn to delegate and some you may just stop doing completely.

The conclusion was that I learned that my two most profitable activities were,

Toolbox   Getting Started

1. Face to face meetings with potential customers
2. Delivering goods/services for actual customers

And the only reason I knew this was because of one further high pay off activity:

3. Planning and Review

This now means that I spend as much of my time working in just these three areas as I continue to grow my business.

Knowing your numbers

> *"If at first it does not work on paper then how can we expect it to work in reality"*

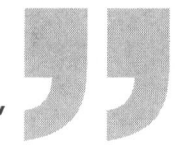

This was a piece of advice that I received early on in my career, and since I have continually taken an analytical approach to growing sales.

Every successful sale is the result of a combination of variables that lead up to that success. Imagine your sales process as a machine and every stage is a component in that machine. Typically, if a machine is not working as it should, it is rarely the whole machine that is at fault, it is simply that one or more of the components are not running efficiently.

By monitoring and measuring we can find the individual areas for improvement and continually work to improve the end result. This will often result in developing some essential Key Performance Indicators (KPIs).

The areas we measure in our sales process are as follows:

- Marketing activity / lead creation
- Lead/ Appointment
- Appointment / Sales conversion
- Average transaction value
- Number of transactions per annum

It was Jim Rohn who said that "if you do something often enough a ratio appears". Once you have found that ratio only then can you improve it.

Chapter 2
Confidence

Success breeds success and keeping a high level of personal confidence is essential to perform at your best. As a sales professional you are a leader. Your customers are looking for your help, advice and enthusiasm to carry them through to decision, and maintaining your self-confidence is paramount in achieving that. If you are not convinced then you certainly can't convince.

What I don't have is the ability to smooth out all the bumps in the road but what I do have is a number of thoughts, tools and processes that can help you build a bigger wheel and ensure that you do all you can to perform at your best.

People buy people

A detailed knowledge of the customers you would like to have, the prospects you are working on and your existing customers, is a necessity in maximising your success. The important thing to remember though is that people buy from people, not organisations.
By researching and understanding what is important to the key decision makers within the business you

are prospecting you will be far better prepared and drastically improve your confidence. Find out their interests, their hobbies and their personal circumstances, as these help you understand about the person behind the job description. The length of time they have been involved in their business, other key decision makers, their competition and their plans for the future are all facts that will give you both increased confidence and the added edge in the marketplace.

It may sound like a drawn out and time consuming process to gather this information, however I promise this information is easily available if you choose to look for it. The internet is full of useful information. Company websites give facts; yet, personal profiles such as Facebook, Linkedin and Twitter often provide a wealth of valuable information. You can also find out great information from the people you know. Contacts within the business can provide valuable information about your prospects and this will bring you a significant competitive advantage. If you receive referrals in your business then please take the time to question your referral source to gather information that may be useful.

Levels of Success

Is every "no" really one step closer to a "yes"?
As a young sales person this mantra was continually

Toolbox   Confidence

drummed into me with a view to dusting myself down and moving on to the next opportunity. Although the psychology behind this is correct, the only thing it really identifies is that to succeed in sales you must maintain a high level of confidence. The truth is- every "no" hurts. We take a no personally and this underlying fear of rejection is one factor that prevents many of us realising what we are capable of.

Not only does this system result in us holding back on opportunities for the fear of rejection, but we can also find ourselves celebrating success before the job is complete. In every successful sale we have ever conducted there would have been more on the table, yet our lack of planning and enthusiastic approach will often result in us wrapping up early and leaving things behind.

My solution for this is to plan out your levels of success before every opportunity. Let me share with you the levels I planned out before a recent opportunity:

1. Give a good representation of myself and my company
2. Build rapport
3. Create a genuine opportunity to introduce our services
4. Give my potential customer enough information to make an informed decision

> 5. Get a decision
> 6. Find out what future opportunities may arise
> 7. Schedule our next action
> 8. Ask for referrals
> 9. Gain a referral

This may sound simple, however, I follow this process before every phone call, business meeting, networking event and speaking opportunity and it serves me so well that it is now part of my routine.

Let's consider how it helps in the following areas...

Confidence
Success in sales is not black and white and very often customers do not make up their mind to do business with us in the first meeting. By understanding which level of success I am at with a prospect I never fail: I have just not succeeded yet!

You will also notice that the first level of success is within your control. Providing that you continually hit this one, the ball is in play and you have already started to succeed. The trick is to understand that no two scenarios are the same and sometimes you will race up these steps in one meeting, whereas on other occasions it will take a long time. However at each point you are winning and this can massively help your confidence.

Toolbox — Confidence

Structure
Planning out your success before you have started can keep you in control and give you direction. It allows you to go through each level one at a time and tick them off in your mind. If you imagine it like you are building some flat packed furniture – I am certain that you have had mixed experience with this – but you will have also had far greater success by following the instructions step by step as opposed to opening all the components and guessing.

Our challenge in sales is that we should re-write out our instructions before every opportunity.

Getting more
You will get more from each opportunity by planning your levels. There will have been several occasions when you have experienced a customer opportunity and then closed the meeting as quick as possible, just in case they change their mind. If you plan out your success past the first sale you have a heightened chance of achieving it. Think about the things that you want to happen after the first positive decision. It may be more business, maybe a referral or two, or perhaps just some further advice. As you will often hear me say,

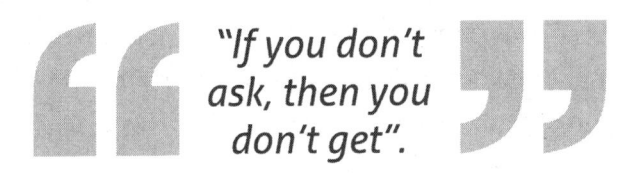

> *"If you don't ask, then you don't get".*

Confidence | Toolbox

It is tough

Running your own business is tough. It comes with a list of challenges and obstacles that many of us never even knew existed before we started in business. It's certainly no easy ride; from the sleepless nights to the cash flow challenges, we have all faced them, and all of us reading this now are still moving forward and still in business.

I don't have a secret formula for overcoming these challenges, but over the years I have learnt some simple skills and techniques that have really helped me to work through them and continue to build a successful business.

1. Take the time to establish WHY you are doing what you are doing. Your business should be your vehicle to help you achieve all that you wish for in life. Write a detailed list of all the things that you wish to have, all the events you wish to experience and all the qualities you wish to possess. In understanding your reasons as to why you are putting in all of your efforts, you will find the determination that will help you plough through those challenging times.

2. Consider who you take advice from. We are all conditioned from the very first moment we're born and those who we spend our time with have a massive impact on our lives. I have countless lessons of this where I have experienced both extremes; from very positive to very negative conditioning. However, the people we need to be most considerate of are those who are closest to us. Our loved ones, our families and our friends, all have significant feelings, and their duty of care and safety is often portrayed by them adding doubt and caution to your plans. As a result of this, I very rarely speak about business with my family as they are conditioned by a very different world.

3. Visualise your achievements. Most of us still have countless items on our never-ending to-do lists. Trying to complete this impossible task can be tiresome, at best, and I often counteract this by considering all the things that I have achieved in my life to date; this includes an achievement list. The things that help me most are often very visual things such as trophies and awards I have won, photos from key moments and framed images of special events that we have delivered. When you receive testimonials please record them and refer back to them. Remembering what you have achieved in the past gives you confidence to counter any self-doubt.

4. Have a mentor. Choosing someone that can bring you their experience, help answer questions, and ask you the questions you are too afraid to ask yourself, is a great aid when dealing with challenging times. Remember that it is your job to choose the mentor rather than them choosing you.

5. Win when you are winning. It is very easy to take your foot off the gas and enjoy the limelight when you reach a level of success. However by continuing to push on when you are in this peak state you will add further success and you will reach levels you did not realise existed.

Making your own luck

Many of us get referrals from contacts and customers to new business opportunities. For most of us this is our preferred method of winning new customers and ideally would be the only way we did business.
The reason a referred opportunity is desired is that it is already a much warmer prospect and your chances of success are significantly higher, so your confidence is high. This success is based on trust. Your success with this opportunity is largely as a result of the quality of the introduction and you are gaining benefit from the trust your prospect has in your referral source.

By doing your homework you can replicate this trust relationship with stone cold prospects by following these simple steps.

Toolbox   Confidence

1. Find out who your prospect already does business with
2. Find out your prospect's fiercest competitor
3. Find out a mutual acquaintance that is well respected, either a local or a national figure

Once armed with this information ensure your meeting includes the following.

1. Start with an open discussion about how you both know, or have an interest in, the mutual acquaintance.
2. During conversation mention the businesses that you work with that are the same as, or similar to, the organisations your prospect works with. If no familiarity then name drop your most recognised contact.
3. Towards the end of the meeting you must subtly elude to a further meeting with their competitor.

By following these simple steps your mutual acquaintance builds rapport and starts to develop trust. Your relationship with like-minded business reinforces that trust and finally your acknowledgement of their competition provokes the biggest decision catalyst of all- fear of loss.

Confidence Toolbox

Your competition

Having competitors is essential to perform at your best; nobody wants to win a one horse race, so understanding who you are competing with dramatically affects your posture in the marketplace.

Take the time to explore how you are similar to your competition and what you do that is different. Look at what makes you unique. Many businesses talk of their unique selling point (USP) and it can often be something that is not truly unique.

If you wish to appear different from your competitors then you must demonstrate and act that you are different.

Conduct a SWOT Analysis on each of your competitors and find out exactly how you can out-manoeuvre them and grow your market share.

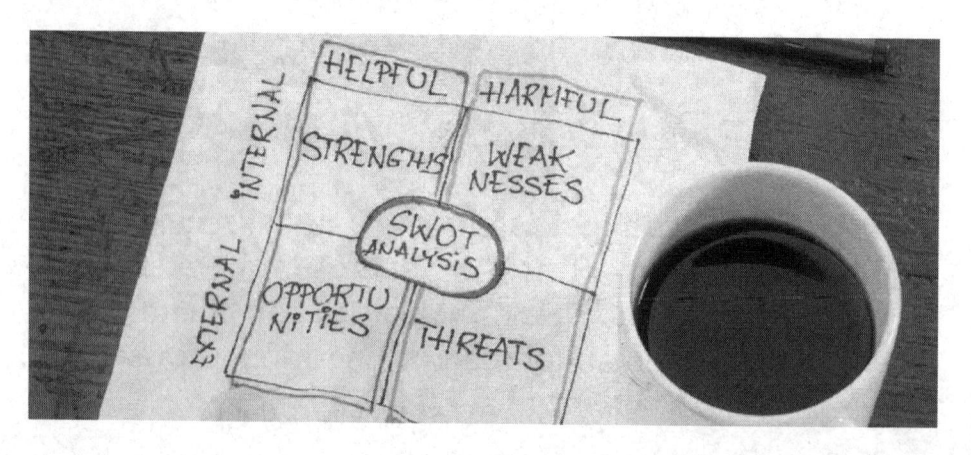

philmjones.com

Toolbox   Confidence

Your competition are incredibly valuable and allow you to position yourself alongside them. To be respected by your customers never de-value yourself by down talking your competitors, simply talk about what they do and what you do better.

Chapter 3
Opening doors

The most common challenge I am presented with is that businesses are looking for more of the right people to speak to. Provided that you have followed the advice in the first chapter you should now have a comprehensive list full of people to do business with. You should have planned your levels of success and be ready to get to work. I believe that the true challenge is to understand how to get in front of more of the right people.

In this chapter we explore numerous techniques to do exactly that.

10-5-2

On my travels I am often asked how to find more of the right type of prospects, so that time can just be spent with people looking to buy and not with time wasters. People try targeted advertising campaigns and volume direct mail to create opportunity; however, they are often disappointed with the response rate and the realisation that there is no short cut to success.

Yes these techniques have their place and each bring a level of success, however my biggest concern with these larger campaigns is not that they may not have the success rates anticipated, but more that if they do work then the business may not be in the position to service the response.

When I question business owners looking for more customers the desired growth rate in relation to number of a customers is often a very sensible number. In most circumstances just 1 or 2 new customers a week would revolutionise a business. What could 100 new customers do for your business?

If this is a level of growth you are serious about then I have a tried and tested strategy that will guarantee success. Before I share it with you please let me explain my three key concerns with all forms of traditional marketing:

1. They all go looking for people who have already decided they are interested in your product and service, and hence have a strict brief for their requirements.
2. People will typically shop around and hence you do not have an exclusive opportunity
3. There is no control of the results

Toolbox   Opening doors

With this in mind, the job of persuading our prospects that they should do business with us can become extremely difficult, as they have too many pre-conceived ideas.

My route to market is completely different. I believe that there is no fast track to the perfect opportunities and often the missing ingredient to the success you desire is a little extra activity and a lot more direction, so I urge you to try my simple technique for just 4 weeks and then measure the results.

> *Grab your prospect list with at least 100 names on it*
>
> *Make phone calls to arrange appointments with as many contacts as possible from your list. The purpose of the appointment is local business owner to local business owner to have 15 minutes together over coffee and see how you can help each other.*
>
> *You will get at least ten appointments. In these appointments please first establish how you can help them. Then ask questions to establish what requirements they have for what you do and look for simple solutions. Do not try to sell to them. You are simply looking to establish if there is a genuine business opportunity there.*

At least 5 of your meetings will highlight a requirement for what you do. Then say these words... "I am not sure if it is for you, but, do you know anyone who..." and introduce your products and services. By introducing your business in this way it is completely rejection free and makes it easy for your prospect to answer.

If done right then at least two of your prospects will buy from you. However the good news in doing it this way is that those who don't buy will typically pass you to someone else who may do. They find it easier to pass you on rather than give you a reason why they don't want to buy. You then simply start the process again.

The trick to this method is to simply get the appointment without being too prescriptive. Yes, you have a lot of meetings, however, if two new customers a week could change your business, then getting 10 appointments a week is surely worth it. They typically take less than an hour and you may just find it is your very best investment of just 10 hours a week.

Networking for success

When many of us are looking for new business we can find ourselves in the mysterious world of business networking,

Toolbox — Opening doors

but for most, attending open networking events is a less than enjoyable experience. We all know that to find new customers we must speak with more people, so why do so many of us find this such a daunting task?

The reason we find this difficult is that we were all conditioned as children by a simple sequence of words- "Don't talk to strangers!". The first challenge is to defy that conditioning and I've found that the easiest way to resolve this is to understand that pretty much everybody else is feeling the same as you.

Getting over the initial 'fear' is one thing, however, to succeed in a network here are some simple rules that have worked for me, and I am sure if you choose to employ them they could have significant benefit to you too.

> **1. Have a plan**. Regardless of the size of the event, it is unlikely that you can develop lasting business relationships with all in the room, and I am certain that there will be some people who will be of considerably more value than others. Set a goal and stick to it. It may be to make a number of new connections, or to set a meeting with a specific person. Just turning up to see what happens is leaving your success to chance.
>
> **2. Know what you are going to talk about.** Starting a conversation is the hardest thing to do when entering

a room full of strangers. To open conversation, the easiest place to start is by talking about a subject that you all have in common. The one subject that you all have in common is the event you are at. As such, plan a series of questions related to the event.

3. Talk of how you help people. "So what do you do then?" This is a question that you are almost guaranteed to be asked, yet each time I witness it the receiver of the question looks startled and bemused, and hesitantly gives their job title or profession as the answer. Your goal from this question is to open a conversation by being interesting to them. So when asked this question please re-phrase it in your head to "How do you help people?" and answer that question instead.

4. Sell to the room. This goes against what you are often told when networking, yet is based on the simple reality that your best referrals come from existing customers. Therefore to gain a quantity of referrals you need a good number of customers within your network. Now, this does not mean forcing your products or services on people, but simply having a simple entry level offering that makes it easy for people to experience what you do.

By utilising some, if not all, of the above tips I am sure you will reap significant returns. Good luck in your networking!

Questions for a room full of strangers

1. What bought you here today?
2. How do you know <name>?
3. Where have you travelled from today?
4. What are you hoping to get out of this event?
5. Have you been here before?
6. Do you attend many events like this?
7. How are you enjoying the event?
8. What type of people are you hoping to meet today?

What face are you wearing?

Building rapport is a crucial skill when you are looking to attract new customers and it starts with one simple action that is often overlooked. The first thought someone makes when they meet you for the first time is "Do I find you attractive?" and we are all proven to be more attractive when we are smiling.

The wondrous thing about a smile is that it is infectious. If you smile at someone, they can't help but smile back! Think back to the times you have been dating in the past or, dare I say it, flirting. This all starts with a smile. Smiling is the best ice-breaker we have when starting new relationships and it is rarely laboured enough to enforce its impact in the sales process. We don't just smile with our mouths – a smile can be transferred in so many ways.

> *Facial expressions* – Smiling is something that we do with our whole face. We have all seen a child's face on Christmas morning – this is the best example of a complete smile. How often are you wearing yours?

> *Body language* – Understanding that we smile with our whole body is a key lesson when attracting people to you. Open body language and a positive stance will attract people to you.

> *Voice* – Anyone who sells or has bought over the telephone will know that you can hear a smile. In the first few seconds of a call you can hear the warmth in the voice which allows you to make an instant decision on your like or dislike of the person.

Company image – I believe it is also important to consider the "Smile" your whole company makes. From your logo, to your dress code, to the way you answer your phones - all demonstrate your company's personality and all can help to attract new customers.

You are probably thinking that you are a pretty happy person most of the time ... Sometimes we just forget to tell our faces!

As creatures of habit, reminders to turn on our "happy face" when we are in the market place can be the nudge we need to smile more. When I speak on stage, I remind myself to smile by writing the word across the top of my notes. When we opened Debenhams stores, we put mirrors on the doors that opened onto the shop floor with signs saying "smile you are on stage." What prompts do you have to make to ensure you are showing yourself at your best?

Who is the most important person?

The most important person in your life is YOU. To test this, remember back to your school group photographs

Opening doors   Toolbox

and ask yourself who is the first face that you look for? Establishing this is essential because people do business with people who they know, like and trust.

Building this trust will rarely come from anything you say about yourself but will largely come from how you make people feel.

All decisions are made with emotion before logic and the result we are looking for is that it "feels right" to do business with you. The most successful approach you can take, to make progress in this area, is to understand that your prospect is the most important person in their life and you simply have to show a genuine interest in them.

This means you must ask questions and listen. You must refrain from using their answer to a question to educate them on your similar experience, and you must simply ask further questions to reveal the details of their answers.

By listening intently you are demonstrating that they are important to you and this will help towards them feeling good. The profession that I continually see do this, better than most, is ladies hairdressers. They continually show interest in their clients and encourage them to talk about themselves. The result of this is increased customer loyalty and further referrals. You can demonstrate that you are listening in a number of ways and I would encourage you to nod and periodically repeat back to them what they have said. You will also find that by maintaining eye contact and not speaking will encourage them to continue talking and share even more information.

What's in a name?

The sweetest sound to any person anywhere in the world is the sound of their own name. We all know this, but many of us forget the importance, and continually struggle to remember the names of others.

The main reason that we struggle to remember names is because we never heard them in the first place. Often too busy wondering what you are going to say, or being distracted, the thought of remembering their name stays too low down the list to be important.

You must start by deciding that remembering their name is important and make sure that you are actively listening for it to give yourself a chance to recall it. Once you have heard it, your brain needs a system to store that information, so you can recall it easily when required.

A long time ago, my good friend and mentor, Peter Lee, introduced me to a name memory system using the acronym ARI. This has served me well and I will share it with you, but will start by giving you some important background information.

Most importantly you must understand that our memory works best by recalling images and not words. Obviously a name is a word so the whole purpose of ARI is to find a way of turning a name into an image.

Secondly, it is important that you understand that we have both a long term and a short term memory. If you choose to place the name in your short term memory then it will not be available for too long. Place it in your long term memory and you have more chance of recalling it when required.

Therefore ARI works by attaching names to images that already exist in your long term memory.

> **A**ssociation – When you meet someone for the first time and greet them in some way, listen to their name and then associate it to someone you already know with the same name. Simply imagine that in meeting this new person you are greeting someone you can recall easily to mind, perhaps a friend or family member, or a famous person who shares the same name. This works with both first names and surnames and the more vivid the image you create the more likely you are to remember it. You can associate to people, places or objects and can create a picture that you later recall.

Toolbox   Opening doors

Repetition - Our memory works better the more we practice. I learnt my times tables by continually repeating them time and time again until the information sticks. The same applies with name memory- you must use names back in your dialogue to improve your chances of recalling it when required.

Impression - There are countless times when I have met someone in an unfamiliar context, perhaps in a shopping centre or at a social function, and they clearly knew me, yet I have struggled to recall how I know them. The reason for this is that I had chosen to remember something about them that can change easily. People often change their clothes, hair, make-up and accessories and all of these can drastically change their appearance. By impression, I mean that you focus your memory on a part of them that is unlikely to change too much, their face. Imagine a passport size photo or avatar of just their face and attach an impression of that image in your memory.

All of these techniques help to remember names, but none of them work without practice. I encourage you to practice this at every opportunity and you will be amazed of the impact it can make.

Making yourself more memorable

We have established that remembering names is not easy but will have an impact on your success. What else will contribute is making yourself more memorable to your marketplace.

I learnt a very simple trick from a fabulous trainer called Sue Tonks who is a very experienced business networker. Sue taught me that when introducing yourself you should give your name twice. Firstly you should give your preferred method of being addressed, followed by your full name including surname. Therefore I introduce myself as "Phil, Philip Jones" and therefore give others two opportunities to catch my name. It is simple but it really works.

Treat them as your best customer

There is a lot that we can all learn about customer service, but most of it is aimed at delivering great service after you have secured the customer. I believe that if you treat each of your potential customers as

Toolbox | Opening doors

your 'best' customer, there is every chance they will become your best customer.

What I do know about this area is a really critical piece of advice that was first introduced to me by one of the most inspirational people that I have ever met, my Nan. My Nan taught me that the most important factor to remember is that "it is the thought that counts". I have this mantra running through my head in so many scenarios and it reminds me of the little things that make huge differences, so here are just a few that I can think of right now.

- Praise and complement others
- Offer support in times of trouble
- Random acts of kindness
- Remembering to say thank you
- Opening doors for others

My secret weapon

In all my years I have tried and tested countless methods of catching people's attention, creating opportunities and winning more business. I have spent time and money developing detailed marketing plans to help open doors but, to date, I have one method that stands head and shoulders above everything else.

Opening doors | Toolbox

Understanding that "it is the thought that counts" I wanted to find out the one form of communication that would guarantee my message is received, be high impact and deliver results.

The result of these thoughts is that I developed this:

This simple piece of high quality, printed and folded card has delivered £1000's in revenue to me as a universal tool to communicate with potential customers.

This card has so many uses and throughout this book I will share many of these with you. However, when it comes to opening doors, simply sending a well thought out hand

Toolbox Opening doors

written message in one of these cards, delivered in a hand written envelope with a first class stamp, will guarantee to capture your prospect's attention.

Please take a look at an example of the card that I sent recently to secure a very significant opportunity.

Sample copy:

> Dear David,
>
> I have long been an admirer of your business and the great work that you do.
>
> I believe that I have a lot to offer the future success of your business and would love to talk further.
>
> I will be in touch shortly to see how we can help each other.
>
> Thanks a million
>
> Phil

The other incredibly important difference between a card and a letter is that cards stand up and get displayed and letters end up getting filed. This results in one being a referral generation tool for your business and the other having very little impact.

The phone call

Following a card of this nature should be done with one purpose in mind, winning a face to face appointment. The call should be friendly, short and direct. It should also happen around 2 days after your card arrives, giving them chance to read it and check you out. Don't be surprised if they call you first!

Social Media 3 step plan

Technology continues to move at such a rapid pace and staying ahead of the game is a continual challenge to all of us. The biggest change in the way we now communicate globally is the revelation of social media. Its impact has been so huge that we can now communicate across the planet with such ease, that our marketplaces have increased significantly and our networks are now much easier to reach.

Toolbox   Opening doors

For those unaware of what the term 'social media' relates to, it is the collective term of platforms such as Facebook, Linkedin, Twitter and YouTube and these forms of media are changing the way that we now communicate. This shift in communications sounds drastic, and for many we are fearful of change - particularly when there is technology involved.

Social media is just modern day "word of mouth" and is little different to what you have always done. This is about building relationships with your customers and community, as well as understanding what others are saying about you, to build your brand and grow your business.

One thing I am not is an expert on this subject. However, I have used social media to create results for both my own business and for clients, and I am happy to share those lessons with you. Regardless of the platforms that you use, and how technologies evolve, I am certain that my simple 3 step principle will continue to apply.

> **1. First Impressions Count** – Just like in the real world; you never get a second chance to make a first impression when it comes to social media. Before you open for business I would seriously recommend that you take the time to complete your profiles fully.

Ensure that all biographies and details are current and represent you correctly.

On all platforms the visual appearance is also critical. You can use certain areas to apply your brand identity and convey your business message - this can be done simply and easily by speaking with your designers to create the correct sized artwork.

Consider your photography. These are social platforms, so images should be warm, friendly and not too corporate. I believe these should always include the image of a person, not just a company logo.

2. Build Audience – Once you are all set up most people start to worry about their outbound content. Your content and posts are important, yet only when people are listening. Social media is particularly useful as a communication tool to the people that already know you, so start there.

If using it for business, then your first action should be to connect with as many of your existing customers and contacts as possible. You can do this by uploading your contacts as a database and sending out an invitation. Additionally you should look to use all current communication tools to let people know that you are active on social media. This means adding social media icons to your e-mail signature and stationery, informing all your customers when you write to them, making it a news story on your website and adding leaflets or posters in the view of your customers to entice them to your profiles.

Physically getting your customers to connect with your profiles is harder than just asking. Running a competition or great offer to reward them for visiting your profiles, and connecting with you, will drastically improve your chances. Remember that investing in this audience is critical in achieving social media success, as without an audience your great work could be wasted

3. Be interesting – When it comes to content the key is to remember that these are social platforms. Very few people are enjoying times on social media because they want to be sold to. To be interesting you need to be varied with your communication and show yourself as human. If your message becomes monotonous you become boring and people stop listening, so keep your outbound content varied. For me this means posting in three areas:

- Commenting on, or sharing, useful information relating to your wider industry as a whole.

Opening doors Toolbox

- Presenting your products and services but only with customer focussed offers relating to the action that precedes the sale and not the sale itself. For example; if you are a car retailer you should provide an offer to get people to visit the showroom and not an offer to buy the car.
- Be human. To succeed in Social Media you must be prepared to share some personal information. Life and family events, as well as successes and failures, are great ways of starting dialogue.

Please remember the aim of posting content is to start a conversation or encourage debate. Starting conversation with your contacts opens you up to their contacts and then your network grows.

Magic Words – You couldn't do me a favour

It continues to amaze me how simple words in the English language can have such a massive impact and one of these words is the request for a favour. Whenever you are in communication with someone and ask them for a 'favour' their auto response is typically "yes" before even considering the request that may follow. This simple psychology can be a fantastic tool in the market place and when looking for actions from others is a great way of getting people committed before the details are provided. The request of a favour now takes a major part in my strategies of winning new business and is particularly useful when asking for referrals or creating opportunities to talk to existing contacts about new products and services.

Social Proof

Many of us are great at what we do and the very fact that you are reading this demonstrates your desire to continue to grow. However, many of us do a great job of keeping our fantastic track record a secret from our potential customers.

Sporting greats are judged by what they achieve, and clubs recruit new managers based on their previous results. The same can be said when looking for new suppliers. If you can demonstrate that you have done a fantastic job for others in the past, it goes a long way towards suggesting you will do a good job for them too.

This is more than having testimonials hidden away on your website, in a filing cabinet or in folder in your

Opening doors Toolbox

bottom drawer, along with your customer letters. In today's age, social proof is one of the best convincers you have and growing your social proof can be a huge contributor in helping you win more business.
Now, the distribution of your social proof is important. Before you can showcase it you must ensure that you collect it. The trick here is quite simply "if you don't ask then you don't get". We are all busy people and taking the time to say nice things about each other, in a usable way, is rarely top of the list; therefore, we have to help jump it up the list.

Asking after you have delivered your product or service is likely to bring you a better response than after that moment has passed. Asking in a format that makes it easy for them is also highly likely to bring a better return. The two forms that have worked well for us are video and of course, Linkedin.

Just asking will bring you huge results, but being prepared will help even further. The ability to record video on the spot will have you leaps ahead of your competition and asking at every opportunity will give you heaps of great videos to showcase what others say about you.

Once you get good at asking you will have so much content that you'll want and need to get in front of people. This is some of the stuff that we do which has had fantastic results, and could work for you too:

Toolbox   Opening doors

- Point people from emails to your Linkedin profile to read recommendations
- Leave written testimonials in a folder in the reception area of the office
- Photograph written testimonials and posted on your Facebook page
- Distribute video testimonials across the social networks
- Encourage others to post their positive comments openly on social media
- Update your website testimonials as often as possible and ensure they are easily visible
- Utilise the words of others in marketing literature

A simple lesson, in all of the above, is to put your social proof in front of as many people as possible. However, the real trick is to ensure that every testimonial can be traced back to its source.

Ensuring that your future customers can see the credibility, in the source of your social proof, will add to its effectiveness, which is the bit that makes it all worthwhile.

Opening doors Toolbox

A simple script for asking for testimonials

> "Hi (Insert name), I was wondering if you could do me a massive favour? (Pause and wait for positive response)
>
> If you are happy with the work that we have done for you then I would be delighted if you would be kind enough to take a few moments and share it in writing? (Await positive response)
>
> Thank you so much for that. We will obviously look to use your words in our marketing and share them with potential new customers and I look forward to reading your comments soon.

Another referral generation tool

Gaining referrals is a delightful way of winning new business and creating opportunity. Many people simply wait and hope for referrals but do very little to generate them.

Receiving testimonials is fantastic but there is a lot to gain from writing them too. For each testimonial you write the chances are that it may be used in their marketing, placed in a folder or better still framed and displayed on their reception wall. Take time to consider your words, ensure that whoever is reading it knows enough about you, to see if they could benefit from your product or service.

Fishing in the same pond

High on the priority list of every business growth campaign is the acquisition of new customers. Finding new, qualified prospects is one of the most difficult parts of the sales process and to conquer this there are many ways that we can fast track this process. I am not sure about you, but if there is a slow and difficult way to finding more customers, versus a quicker and more rewarding way, I know which one I would pick…

The tactic in question is the approach of developing strategic alliances. This is working coherently with like-minded businesses that have the same target market as you, yet are typically not in competition.

Forming strategic alliances has been an essential tool in developing businesses and the lesson was served strongest when developing our property business. We had an investment property product that was an alternative to a pension, which resulted in a fair size investment to be made by the customer for some significant long term rewards. Finding people for this product using traditional advertising and digital media was inconsistent, at best, which bought very unpredictable results. This led us to consider which business professionals had access to a good number of our target customers. Defining our target market brought the understanding that our potential customers were typically successful business owners and high salaried employees that were already valuable customers of Financial Advisors, Accountants and Solicitors.

This allowed us to change our sales process entirely and take control of our results, by forming countless small partnerships with these professionals, who could introduce us to their customer base. Just imagine the difference it would make to your business if you were receiving tens of referred appointments with personal recommendations...

Achieving this is within your control if you follow some simple steps:

> **1. Define your target market** - Understand exactly who your ideal customer is and hence what their current spending habits are.
>
> **2. Identify potential partner industries** - Take

care to consider all avenues of potential product and service providers that already have a trusted relationship with your target market.

3. Make a list - List the names and contact details of the people in the organisations that you would like to speak with.

4. Create a win/win scenario – Successful strategic alliances will only work if both parties are happy with the rewards for the effort. Financial reward is only one form of motivation so consider what else you have to offer. Expertise, data and introductions are all immensely valuable.

5. Create appointments to build relationships – Get face to face with the people who you are looking to refer you and your business. We would always prefer to introduce a human than an organisation. It is more rewarding for the introducer.

6. Look for first action – It is easy when discussing potential alliances to get excited by the big picture. The idea will then "grow legs" and will soon become a massive job. Experience tells me that if you make the change too significant nothing will happen. As such, start with something small, I would typically look for just the first introduction.

Opening doors Toolbox

7. Communicate like a pro – When you receive introductions you must understand that you are being trusted with someone else's most valuable asset. Act accordingly and communicate with your introducer every step of the way.

8. Say "Thank You" – Two of the nicest words to hear in the English language are "Thank You" take time to show your sincere gratitude for each introduction you are passed regardless of results.

9. Over deliver - Whatever you promise to your introducer you must over deliver on. A big goal is to get the contact introduced to thank your introducer for the introduction. If you can gain this result then expect a good number of further introductions.

Start thinking today about who could be passing you a steady stream of business? Given the choice of finding customers one at a time, or utilising someone else's hard work and receiving them in multiples, like I said, I know what option I would choose.

Magic Words – If ..... Then

I am always intrigued as to how simple changes in language use can drastically affect the result of communication. In sales, we are often looking to win people round to our way of thinking and help them to make their mind up. Through years of practice I have developed simple sets of words that have guaranteed results. One of these sets of words can help ensure that whoever you are communicating with believes and trusts, with complete conviction, the outcome that you are going to present them with.

The magic words are simply "if" followed by "then". You form a conditional sentence using these words in this sequence, allowing you to place an action after "if" letting your prospect to believe that the result that follows "then" is highly likely to occur.

Examples from childhood would include

> *If you don't eat your dinner... Then you won't get any pudding*
>
> *If you are not back home by 10pm... Then you will be grounded for a week*
>
> *If you don't take the time to revise... Then you won't get good grades at school*

Although the results that follow "then" are not always completely accurate, the success is achieved from the belief that the result will happen. My experience from the above examples was that the "then" was so strong that I certainly did not want to take the risk!

Taking this into your business can allow you to make profound statements and influence consumers in a considerable way. Simple examples would include:

- If you take the time to implement these lessons... Then you will be blown away with the results
- If you attended our one day workshop... Then I promise you won't be disappointed

Getting this working in your daily sales language and written copy will start to win you more business, so - if you are looking for more customers,then you really should try these techniques.

Become the expert

If you are looking to create more opportunities, open more doors and create a barrage of inbound enquiries then you must be seen as the 'expert' in your field. The word 'expert' may make you feel uncomfortable and we wonder how we could possibly position ourselves as such. Surely we haven't studied enough, learnt enough, or we simply don't know enough to be perceived as the expert. But this thinking is flawed because becoming the expert is easier than you think. Dr Joanna Martin taught me that one of the fastest ways to be perceived as an expert is to start delivering presentations on your subject.

What is even more fantastic is that not only are you automatically perceived as the expert once you stand on stage, you also have an audience of multiple potential customers allowing you to create instant leverage.

There are many platforms from which you can share a powerful message that will have you be seen as the expert:

- Speaking at seminars and networking events
- Running teleseminars or webinars
- Participating in radio or television interviews
- Delivering podcasts
- Producing You Tube videos

All of these media platforms are areas where you can start delivering effective presentations, in order to build your position as an expert in your area, but also to increase your sales.

Bin the brochure

So many businesses continue to produce printed flyers and brochures to support their sales force. I have no doubts that in certain industries a product catalogue is an essential tool in the sales process. However in many scenarios what is intended as an aid can become a hindrance.

In place of a brochure I would look to offer something of value to your potential customer. Something that demonstrates what you do and how you help your customers as opposed to telling them what you do. Examples of great brochure alternatives would be:

- An audio CD product
- A sample pack of products
- A book or report written or compiled by you

All of these should deliver value to your potential customer, not be thrown away and should encourage them to take the next step with you. Get this right and your brochure alternatives will be forwarded by your customers to others.

Chapter 4: Winning Appointments

For many of us our business is won from getting face to face with potential customers. We know that we get our best results when we are in front of others, yet the challenge of appointment creation still remains. Through the years we have had continued success in this area and in this chapter I will share with you what has worked for me.

Just pick up the phone

It may sound remarkably simple, but to be honest this is still my most productive approach in winning appointments with people at all levels in a business. Whether winning an appointment with a CEO of a large corporate company, wanting to interview a successful business leader from Accelerator, or secure a new partner for our business, just picking up the phone works for me more often than not.

Please finish this sentence:

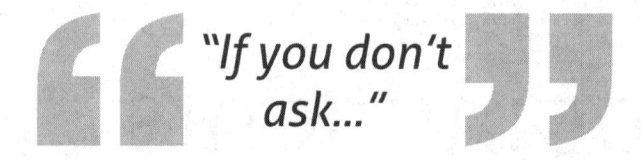

> *"If you don't ask..."*

As children we are conditioned not to ask others for anything as it can appear rude and we must wait to be offered.

Although remarkably courteous, this advice has clearly often been misinterpreted and the truth is that you should ask if you want anything. The skill comes from knowing when to ask and how to ask in order to get the best results.

Don't make cold calls

If you are anything like me then the thought of picking up the phone to a complete stranger certainly does not fill me with joy.

Let's look at cold calling logically and agree some unquestionable truths.

Toolbox   Winning Appointments

- The call is quite likely to arrive at the wrong time for the receiver
- The recipient is unlikely to be thinking of purchasing your product or service at that moment
- They don't like receiving calls from strangers that interrupt their day

All of the above mean that your chances of success in this action are stacked against you before you even start, therefore playing the numbers game, rejection will be the norm and your confidence will dwindle with each and every call.

Reading this book right now, I am sure that the right number of new customers can be achieved by thinking a little smarter, only ever calling people when you have a genuine reason to do so and can look to provide a consultative solution. Simply being prepared, and doing your homework, will make a significant difference to your success.

philmjones.com

Let's look back at the list we discussed in the first chapter.

Friends – Your friends are all people that you are in contact with regularly and therefore contacting them by phone should be a regular occurrence, so picking up the phone in a professional context should be little extra challenge. An easy 'rejection free' way of introducing your business to your friends is to ask in the third person. Instead of asking if they are interested, simply ask if they know someone who would be interested. They will often say themselves!

Records – All of the records we have gathered from previous roles and events we have attended, all give us a simple reason to contact people. Simply discuss the one thing you both have in common, the event or organisation that resulted in you acquiring their records.

Industry- Becoming an industry specialist always carries weight when making phone calls. The fact that you have experience of their industry and have worked with similar industries is often motivation enough for them to want to meet with you.

E – marketing – People who have submitted their details to connect with you on-line are very hot prospects and should be treated with respect. Remember to discuss what bought them to your website, before discussing your products or services.

Networking – Appointment creation from networking is straightforward as you are really having small appointments with everyone you meet. Often these meetings are simply a stepping stone to the true sales appointment, so use these events to win decision making appointments, as opposed to selling at the events.

Directory – Phoning people from membership organisations and directories that you are part of is a very simple introduction. You can simply open conversation by discussing the organisation that you are both a part of and move the conversation on from that point.

Same Name – Everyone you thought of in this section will fall into one of the above categories. Just drop them a call and see how you get on.

These will still be challenging calls but by defining an additional reason, or purpose, for the call in addition to introducing your products or services, makes the calls far easier, with less rejection and greater success.

Two versions of yes

My favourite area of the sales process is closing the order and this is an area I take great pleasure in succeeding at. You will often hear me say that the sales process is all about control and how you can steer your prospect through your process to the desired outcome.

This is absolutely true; however, fantastic results can come whilst maintaining control and you give the illusion that the prospect is making the decisions, which makes them feel empowered.

This is best demonstrated by utilising the 'alternative close' through your sales process. In an alternative close you give your prospect a choice of solutions to pick from; however, what is important is that each answer is a good answer for yourself.

In appointment creations a good example would be: "I am free on Tuesday and Friday this week. Which day suits you best?"

In this example the customer feels obliged to either pick one of your suggested days or suggest an alternative themselves and as such, all answers lead to the creation of an appointment.

Toolbox   Winning Appointments

Be precious with your time

Winning appointments with decision makers is often a challenge because they are often busy people and their time is incredibly valuable.

The mistake that many people make when looking to win appointments is that they ask for too long and appear to be too available. Decision makers are often swayed by intrigue, so by being busy, giving the appearance of being in demand, they will be more motivated to see you for fear of missing out.

Then when it comes to offering an appointment you are more likely to win short appointments if you suggest times that indicate the meeting won't take long. So by suggesting meetings at either 10 past the hour or 20 to the hour it is easier for them to find the time to fit you in. When asking for appointments on the hour they need a clear hour to fit you in.

Telephone techniques that work

1. Be happy. Your enthusiasm is infectious and will bring success.
2. Ask if they have time to talk. Obvious, but we often forget.

3. Know the purpose of your call. Decide what you want before you make the call.
4. Speak clearly. Make it easy for your prospect to understand what you want.
5. Be succinct. Keep the call short as peoples' attention wanders over time.
6. Finish with an agreed action. A call is a short presentation and must close by agreeing an action.

Be easy to contact

As well as all the proactive actions we can take to win appointments, if we do good work and market effectively then people will look to contact us to do business. Many businesses, however, are being sabotaged internally by sales prevention officers affecting the ability of potential customers contacting to register interest. Below are a few common examples that I see regularly, that are all so easily avoidable.

- Telephones not answered
- Inappropriate voicemail messages
- Telephone number not easily accessible from website homepage
- Webpage not found easily when searched for

- No contact details available on marketing materials
- Email signatures missing phone numbers

By avoiding these mistakes you will win more business.

Visit the neighbours

A short while ago, my Dad found himself short on business for the first time since starting his business over 30 years prior. Dad runs a local building company and spends most of his time working on residential building projects and in the space of 4 weeks had 4 large jobs cancel or postponed, meaning he went from being busy for a year to having only enough work until the end of the month.

As all of Dad's work came from recommendations, and he had rarely marketed his business, the thought of acquiring new business quickly was alien and quite daunting.

Although the big jobs had dried up, Dad still had plenty of small repairs and simple jobs to do and kept busy doing these. The bigger challenge was that the phone was not ringing often enough and something needed to change.

Winning Appointments   Toolbox

We discussed a simple strategy that meant at each little job he worked on he would simply introduce himself to each of the adjoining neighbours. Instead of pushing his services, he would simply introduce himself, explain it was his van out front and that he was working next door. He would then give his contact details and mentioned that if the van needed moving, or if his team were of any trouble to them at all, to give him a call.

Dad practiced this process continually for a period of a few weeks and before long the neighbours began to request quotations, and opportunities for new business came flooding in.

A very simple practice with incredible results. Easy to do but equally easy not to do!

How to guarantee an appointment

There will always be occasions where winning that appointment continues to seem out of reach. Gatekeepers stand in the way and appointments continue to get re-scheduled. I learnt one very special way of guaranteeing an appointment in any business to business environment.

Toolbox   Winning Appointments

To guarantee an appointment simply become a customer of the company you would like to work with. Once a customer of theirs you become remarkably more valuable to them and they are much happier to sit down with you.

In addition, this also means that it is well worth looking down your supplier list and seeing who could also be a customer of yours. If you can turn your suppliers into customers, it can make for a massively increased value relationship.

Chapter 5: Winning the first sale

Building a business is tough and the acquisition of new customers for many is the hardest part. Once we have secured a new customer we can then find multiple ways of gaining more from them, yet the first sale presents the biggest challenge. Let's explore the tools we use to win that first piece of business.

Who holds the controls?

Many businesses have a huge challenge in their process when it comes to following up quotes or proposals. There are two simple approaches to this topic. The first approach is to explain how, by controlling the process, you will very rarely find yourself needing to chase or follow up. Secondly in the event of finding yourself in a situation requiring follow up, I want to give you some tips to get back in the driving seat.

Winning the first sale   Toolbox

The sales process is all about control and the aim of the game is to be in control throughout the journey and lead your prospect from enquiry through to decision, successfully steering them through the maze.

A common mistake often made is that we try and cheat tried and tested practices by fast tracking. It's easy to believe that our potential customers are looking to make the purchase based solely on price, so on receipt of an enquiry we jump straight to quotation as quick as possible and then look to have a discussion on price. The truth is that people actually buy on value and, before ever buying a product or service, they will typically buy into a person first.

Knowing that people buy from people, the starting point in avoiding difficult follow up scenarios is to start by building a relationship and, where possible, do this face to face. During this meeting you will build rapport and ask questions to equip yourself with the information you need to make a recommendation to your potential customer. It is at this point that simple mistakes are usually made.

The goal is to put yourself in a position where you can deliver your recommendations in person and not by post or email. With this goal in mind, you should arrange the meeting to discuss your findings before leaving the first meeting. This keeps you in control. The easiest way to do this is to give your customer a choice of two dates for your return visit. They will either pick one or suggest an alternative.

On returning with your recommendations, please understand that you need to start near the beginning again. Re-confirm your customer's requirements and then walk them through your recommendations, explaining exactly how you can help them. Your role is to give them all the information they need to make a decision before asking them to take the next step. By inviting people to make a decision on the day, you can eliminate the need for a follow up call.

Avoiding chasing decisions is definitely the goal and I promise that the time you invest in controlling this process at the beginning will reward immensely, in improved conversion rates, and in less time chasing decisions.

However, sometimes you still find yourself faced with outstanding opportunities that you would like to turn into confirmed orders - so here are some simple tips:

>   1. Don't leave voicemail messages. Leaving a message prevents you from calling again.
>
>   2. Open your call by checking they received your recommendations (not quote or proposal).

3. Ask them, "What questions do you have?" The answers they give here put you back in control. Any questions can be answered to lead to a decision. No questions means a decision has been made.

4. If the first form of communication fails, then try something different. Don't harass.

5. If it's worth it then pop back in to see them face to face.

6. Take your offer away by making it time dependent - just like the fear of removing a child's uneaten dinner with a threat of no dessert - limiting your offer can have the same result.

Remember, the biggest reason people do not buy from you is that they remain undecided. Everybody who is stuck in indecision will at some point decide, therefore if your follow up remains unproductive then don't just stop. Continue to communicate by newsletter and diarise an opportunity to make contact again in the future, because at some point their circumstances will change and they may just need your help. Persistency has certainly proved successful for many before us and I am sure it will continue to bear fruit in the future.

Toolbox — Winning the first sale

Easy first "Yes"

Big decisions are hard to make and getting customers to make big decisions can be quite a decision. When a customer is looking for a new supplier, they have many decisions to make, but perhaps the most important question they ask is "why you?" This question is rarely answered before a decision is made. It can often be answered with referrals, testimonials and by reputation. However, you can often speed up the decision making process and win more new customers by making their first step a simple one.

Let me demonstrate with a very simple example that I am guessing is familiar to you as you are reading this right now. I am sure that you will have eaten in a restaurant; a great industry full of examples of easy first yes's. What they are looking to secure is the maximum transaction value per table and so look to sell drinks, appetisers, more drinks, main courses, more drinks, deserts and coffees to all customers. However what they do first is sell table reservations and market key offers to fill those tables. They know that when they fill the tables they have more chance of selling the food and drinks at various stages throughout your stay. Take a look at your process and see if you are trying to sell the whole meal in one go as, just like a restaurant, it is difficult to decide on a pudding until after you have finished your main meal.

Great examples of easy first yes's are low priced initial transactions that turn your prospects into customers, simply and easily. In our business we use open training programmes and seminars, as tools to win credibility, before looking at coaching and consulting solutions, in fact this book is an example of an easy first yes too!

Make it easy to buy

The main function of a sales person is to encourage customers to purchase goods or services. I often refer to sales people as professional "mind maker-uppers" and if we are looking to help our prospects reach decisions, then we really should take a look at our processes and ensure we are doing all we can to make buying a painless process.

Big decisions are always harder to make than smaller ones. As such I would encourage you to look at your paperwork process and pricing structure and ensure that your prospects are not put off or confused by these. Can your existing contract process be replaced with a simple one page form? Can you create simple offers and products within your business and communicate these so that customers can make a quick decision?

Without a doubt, a decision is far easier to make if the fear of loss is removed. For example, in the 1920's a

Toolbox   Winning the first sale

pioneering retail company named Marks and Spencer introduced a "no quibble" returns policy. This action was a key factor in their significant growth and in 2010 was the UK's leading retailer, with over 21 million people visiting the stores each week.

There are a number of actions you can take straight away that may work for your business.

- Money back guarantee
- Free initial period
- No success - no fee
- No contract
- Guaranteed results
- Attractive payment terms

If you are looking for more business I encourage you to remove all obstacles from your buying process and continue to make your own luck.

Magic Words – Most people

Success in sales is all about winning people round to your way of thinking. Typically you are far more educated in your sales process than any of your customers and you can steer them through a lot of decisions by using simple changes in language.

A long while ago I learned that consumers follow the crowds and act like lemmings. As such, they take comfort from following what "most people" do. With this in mind I can encourage you to utilise these two magic words in situations when you want to give your customers the confidence to take the next step.

Examples would be:

"*The way we work with most people is...*"

"*At this stage most people would be choosing one of these two options...*"

"*Most people in your circumstances tend to go for...*"

So that's it. Two simple words that, when utilised in your sales conversations, help people to make decisions. Please enjoy the success these words help you achieve.

Winning language

The words that we use in our sales discussions can all have a huge impact on the success that we achieve. Simple tweaks and subtle changes can make all the difference. I have developed a keen ear to listen for the words that are used and thought I would share some common examples.

Don't say this...	Say this instead...
If	When
But	And
Cost	Investment
Sign	Autograph
Problem	Challenge – Opportunity
Expensive	Premium
Cheap	Value
When I sell	When you own

Put a bow on it

If you provide a service, as opposed to a range of products, it is likely that many of your customers avoid consulting you as they don't know what they want. As service providers, it is important that we think like retailers. If you owned a shop with items that had no prices showing, a browsing customer may assume that everything in the shop is too expensive, but also you run the risk that they would not ask for assistance for fear of embarrassment.

As service providers we must do all we can to make it easy for our potential customers to engage in conversation with us. Imagine yourself again as a retailer. Your aim is to encourage people into your store and increase footfall. Service based industries have the same goal and can use 3 simple techniques.

1 Price primers
Provide examples of a service which explains your total pricing strategy to customers. Major supermarket chains use value products to do this and the automotive industry may use a range of cars.

The process is to simply take a snapshot of one service and put a price on this, as it will educate your audience to your overall pricing strategy. Being proud of this price will demonstrate the value you believe it offers and allow customers to get a feel for your market position.

Simple examples include assisting an accountancy practice to place fixed prices for each of their core services and helping a domestic cleaning company provide a fixed fee for a 3-room package. These uncomplicated one price offers allow people to decide whether or not they can afford you.

2 Bundled offers
I will often work with clients to create collections of products and services that demonstrate great value. What could you bundle? The idea of this process is to increase your average order value and

introduce your clients to services that they would not normally choose.

When putting your bundle together, consider all that you can include, not only the tangible services or products, but also those which add value such as customer care, service expectation, telephone and email support all of which add substance. An example I recently influenced was a 'business in a box' concept for a local design business. This included the design and production of a full complement of stationery, a basic website and brand guidelines package, aimed at new business start ups.

3 Packages

Most people are concerned less with an overall cost and more about how much something will cost each month. As such we can often align our offerings utilising this buying pattern.

Typically, if you can turn a large 'pay in arrears' product or service, into a sustainable pay monthly option, the results are increased profit, improved cash flow and maximum customer retention. If you are not offering your clients a packaged 'pay monthly' service you may well be missing out on a massive opportunity.

Try packaging up your services and imagine making a display of products in a major retail store with your offering. You may just be overwhelmed by the results.

Your sales presentation

Most people believe that this is the most important part of the sales process, however in my experience I believe it to be the least. Now what I would love you to understand is that the sales presentation is nothing to do with having a fabulous company brochure, a beautiful computer presentation or a fantastic company website.

By the time you deliver your presentation, your prospect should be 80% of the way towards making a decision.

Selling is a transfer of enthusiasm. It is creating a ball of energy and passing that to your prospect, so that they are as excited about receiving it as you are delivering it. Being enthusiastic talks straight to the subconscious mind and promotes enthusiasm in return, which then becomes a catalyst to a buying decision.

In theory you should be able to present your products or services with no props, other than a pen and blank piece of paper.

I am not saying that this is the only way you should present. However, if you can do that, you will then only add marketing material that supports your presentation and not hide behind your literature.

Now every successful presentation follows a structure. Be it a quick elevator 60 second pitch, or a detailed half day tender, the same structure applies.

This may sound simple but every presentation should include a beginning, middle and an end. This sounds simple, but the number of presentations that I see that are all middle is still in abundance.

Beginning
Your beginning is really your chance to set the scene and educate that your prospect that your meeting has moved on and they will soon have a decision to make. The two main ingredients for your beginning are always to make a powerful opening statement, to then put your audience at ease by letting them know what to expect by sharing your agenda with them. By giving them a verbal or written agenda they understand what to expect and it helps you to keep control.

Middle
The middle of a presentation is where your main responsibility is to give your audience enough information to make a buying decision. I would always look to consider three main areas.

> *1. Your history and credibility - Let your listeners understand all about you and your company. Share the type of companies that you work with and instil*

confidence in your audience that you are more than capable of delivering for them. This is not a huge section but is vitally important. Drop in names of existing customers and words that others have used to describe you.

2. Product or service overview - Always provide a shopping list of all your products and services in every sales presentation. You never know what they may also be interested in buying from you.

3. The one product/service for them – Finally give them your recommendations for the solution that they make a decision on today. Remember to keep this as simple as possible.

You will need a powerful opening and close to your middle to keep attention. Keep questions to a minimum throughout your sales presentation and if necessary they must be simple, closed and bring positive engaging answers so as not to lose control.

End
Providing your presentation was interesting enough, at some point you will have lost the full attention of those listening. This is because something you said had interested them and they started to think about applying your solutions and may have missed something. Because it is paramount that they feel they have all the

Toolbox   Winning the first sale

information before they make a decision it is essential that you summarise before closing. Your summary is simply telling them what you have told them. Once you have summarised you must then close.

I would encourage you to prepare a default presentation for each of your products and then tailor it each time you need to use it. That way you are always prepared.

Magic Words – Just Imagine

Customers and prospects make buying decisions on emotion and not logic. Decisions are made by the mind painting pictures of the outcomes and then using these images to either attract them towards something or repel them away from something.

To help people make decisions easier we must help them visualise the outcome of utilising your products or service. Two magic words that make it very easy for you to start painting a picture in the mind of your prospect are "Just imagine".

By prefacing sentences with these 2 words It takes the listener back to childhood story time and they very quickly start to visualise the picture that you go on to describe.

These words can be used very effectively to help people see the benefits of taking on board your products or services. They can also be used to paint pictures of more difficult situations that allow prospects to picture themselves in the scenario you paint for them and can then decide how to act. People will only take action for a potential gain, or to avoid a loss. Painting a picture of Utopia, or a difficult situation, will encourage them to make a decision.

Examples would be.

- Just imagine how you feel in the future when you are …
- Just imagine what would happen if you couldn't …
- Just imagine if you didn't do this …
- Just imagine what it will feel like knowing that …
- Just imagine what you could do with an extra £X month …

Building Value – Presenting Price

One of the easiest ways of preventing price objections is to build the value before presenting the price. It's simple psychology in that if you can create the desire, then they will work for a solution, as opposed to trying to justify a price later.

When building value it helps people to look at what it means to them and a price must always have something to be compared to. The process I am referring to is known as the contrast principle and using this ensures your price represents great value when compared to a viable alternative.

Consider how your product or service helps the consumer and question them about what it would mean to them if they were not to have your solution. You are painting the picture of the consequences of them not buying from you, as opposed to the upsides of actually buying from you.

By creating this wide contrast before presenting the benefits of your solution, and in turn your price, your prospect can then truly see the value in your offering. You can contrast against other competitive solutions, yet often the most powerful thing to contrast against is them taking no action at all.

If you don't take the time to deliver this contrast first, then your chances of gaining a decision from that prospect are greatly reduced.

Being Assumptive

Throughout all we have shared so far, we have taught a very consultative sales process. The biggest reason that people don't ask for the business is that they are scared of rejection and fear for the potential customer saying no to them.

During the course of my career, I have used and continue to use a variety of closing tools, yet the one that brings me the most success and is completely rejection free is by closing in an assumptive fashion.

This works so well, because consumers are looking to be lead and most people are not confident when it comes to making decisions. If you are at the point in your communication where you are looking for a decision, an assumptive close would simply make a statement of what the buying decision was and then follow with a simple question that can only be answered once the decision has been made.

It takes confidence and posture to deliver effectively, however please consider all the work you will have done to have got to this point. No doubt, your prospect is very interested and has nodded and smiled all through your presentation. I promise at this point you have earned the right to be assumptive.

A simple example would be:

"We will make a start on your project straight away and your investment is just £450, to get things started I have a simple one page form to complete that starts with your name and address?"

If they answer the question then they must have agreed to the statement proceeding and have therefore confirmed the order.

The only action your customer can take by alternative is to ask you a question. If they do, simply answer the question and then reiterate your simple closing question.

Closing sentences that work

- What is going to be easier...?
- Which one suits you best?
- Is (quantity) enough for you?
- Most people would now...
- Will the (Insert date) be soon enough for you?

Dealing with faffers

I am sure that you have had times in your career where you have had dealings with people where you just can't get a decision from them. Perhaps they have asked you to revise your proposals time and time again and have been in your 'maybe' pile for what seems like an eternity.

I refer to these people as "faffers" and it is our job to bring these people to a decision, quickly and efficiently. Our time is precious and in these scenarios the direct approach is really the best option. I would only ever use this approach if I am comfortable in receiving a "no" response from the prospect.

This means simply presenting them with a "Yes" or "No" option with phrases like "Are you going to place an order? yes or no?"

Your confidence in this process will trigger a decision and either way you can move forward. This can often result in a positive decision as the fear of you taking the offer away can regularly trigger a buying decision.

Too much of a good thing

One of the most common mistakes in the sales arena is overselling. You will have all heard the old saying the plan is to under sell and over deliver. It is interesting that although we still believe the above to be true, we can still continue to keep adding products and promises to our proposition in order to make our offer more compelling.

The truth in this tactic is that it is destined to failure, for two reasons:

> **The promises that we make, in association to the prices that we present, do not add up and therefore the result is that we deliver less than expected and have an unsatisfied customer. Or we provide too much work for too little pay and the work becomes non-profitable.**
>
> **Consumers are conditioned to believe that if something sounds too good to be true, then it probably is.**

The first of these points is self explanatory, so it is the second that I would like to focus on now. If, as human beings, we are conditioned that the more we embellish something the less we believe it to be true, then surely we must find a way of making our sales presentations more believable.

When things sound 'too good to be true' the question we ask ourselves is "where is the catch?" To resolve this issue and win people round to our way of thinking, there are some simple solutions:

> **1. Tell them the catch**. With every transaction there is some bad news to go with all the good news. If you share the bad news also, it helps people see your offer for exactly what it is.
>
> **2. Be proud of your price**. Not being proud of your price suggests that you don't believe it offers value. The more confident you are in your price the more the consumer believes it is a fair price to pay.
>
> **3. Set their expectation levels realistically** - work off a minimum level of expectation and then go out and over achieve for your clients. By taking this approach you will not only win more business, but maintain your customers for longer periods, because you will typically be exceeding expectations.

Have a down-sell

You have no doubt heard of business having a range of upsells. At the start of this chapter, I reiterated that customer acquisition is the most difficult action of all areas of business growth. It is therefore useful to look for ways of capitalizing on all those scenarios where we don't get the primary result we are looking for, in a sales scenario.

When unsuccessful in securing your initial outcome, consider what you could introduce as an alternative. This may mean resorting to an "easy first yes" or perhaps even just a small part of the anticipated order.

What I do know is that part success is far more satisfying than complete failure, and having the agility to introduce smaller decisions if your first action fails will bring significant additional business to you.

Many of our customers that are unable to attend our live events will invest in a lower priced home study version as an alternative. That way we still gain a customer and they still gain the material they are looking for, and both parties win. By not having a down-sell you will create many scenarios where both parties lose.

Buying triggers

There are many factors that trigger people into making buying decisions and some of the best that have worked for me include.

- Scarcity of product
- Limited offer
- Ease of first action
- Free gift with purchase
- Quantity discount
- Attractive payment terms
- Speed of delivery
- Removal of fear of loss

Chapter 6
Maximising opportunities

Gaining the first order is only part of the process. Amplifying your profit possibilities will come from increasing your average order values, ensuring your customers come back time and time again. In this chapter we fill your toolbox with tried, tested and proven strategies, to get the most out of all that you do.

What are you leaving on the table?

Every one of us is missing sales and business growth opportunities every single day.

Whether from face to face appointments, telephone conversations or marketing messages, we are bi-passing huge potential for enhancing our sales success.

I can imagine that a number of you are challenging what I have just said, in your mind right now, and consider that your sales conversion rates are high and business is buoyant. This, however, is not about being competent, or just above average, it's about taking each and every opportunity and maximising it.

For many of us, we simply have two potential outcomes from a sales opportunity; success or failure. What I am asking you to consider is to remove the option of failure and replace it with different levels of success, this is about "raising the bar".

What this means is you need to plan your levels of success before each opportunity and consider what there really is on offer. You might have an appointment with someone who has shown an interest in one particular product or service. If you open your mind, think; what else could this person provide you with? Things to consider are as follows:

> **Additional sales** - The easiest time to sell something else to someone is immediately after making the first buying decision.

> **Further appointments** - Increasing the frequency of transaction, is a fantastic way to grow a business and planning the next appointment keeps you in control of this.

Referrals - Asking for referrals should be part of your daily routine

Cost Savings - If you spend with these people too, they may be able to improve their offer to you. If you don't ask then you certainly don't get.

A cheeky request – Many of your customers will have a database of customers and send them regular newsletters. If you ask to be included in this they may well agree. Again, if you don't ask then you don't get!

So please consider where your bar is set for your sales opportunities. Consider what success looks like to you and go and achieve more of what you are capable of.

Magic words – Enough

You are probably starting to realise now that I enjoy how simple changes in words can have dramatic differences on results. For any of us who sell on frequency or quantity, the introduction of the word "enough" can sky rocket your average transaction value. Providing you're reasonable, the word 'enough' allows you to maximise your order value and stretch your customer's spend. A recent example is with a printing customer of mine, who typically sold stationery in multiples of 500. By asking "Is 1000 letterheads enough for you?" during sales presentations he has now doubled the size of his average stationery order. Simple - but very effective.

Prod the bruise

Questions are so important in stopping you guessing and ensuring that you earn the right to recommend your products and services. Typically the reason for any sales opportunity not being maximised is that the questions were either missing or inappropriate.

Understanding that people make buying decisions based on emotion and not logic, it is paramount that you get your prospect to share emotion during your questioning. A tried and tested approach to nearly every sales opportunity is to follow this simple 3 stage questioning technique.

1. What is your plan...?
I would always start with the biggest possible question I can. In my business I typically start by asking quite simply "So explain to me the plan for the business?" The result of this question is often 15 minutes of communication that give me the big picture and

includes the business owner's goals. The key is to keep the question broad and not specific. Your product offering will only affect part of the plan, however not understanding all of it makes it difficult to understand where your bit fits in. I am looking for detail and drawing towards emotion as often as possible. In this series of questions I am looking first for the 'what?' and then the 'why?'. If the plan includes luxuries- get specifics, as these become very valuable when closing.

2. How will you feel…?

Once you understand where they are going its important to understand how they will feel when they get there. This is simple; you just need to ask … And then listen. You will need to dig a little here to get to the real emotions that make this technique really powerful. You are looking to evoke extreme emotions like pride and euphoria. Encourage strong adjectives and don't accept simple answers like "I will feel pretty good" or "ok".

3. What are the consequences of not…?

Steps 1 and 2 I am sure are familiar with many of you already, however this third question is the one that really hits the button. It's true that we are more motivated to avoid a loss than make a gain. Knowing this I evolved this questioning technique to finish here, as it finds where your prospects pain is and gives you the chance to agitate it a little. Most people don't give sufficient consideration to failure and asking this question forces them to think about it. Once people have visualised failure they will avoid it at all costs.

This technique works by simply establishing the plans of your prospect, elaborating the success of achieving these plans and then visualising the pain of failure. I often describe it as painting Utopia for them, checking their feelings and then finding their bruise and aggravating it a little. The good news is that once you have prodded the bruise enough, your presentation should be the best ointment for that bruise, and if you get these processes right you will win more business.

Great questions allow you to stop selling and start recommending.

Peeling back the layers

In the highly acclaimed animated movie production, Shrek, there is a scene where Shrek announces that Ogres are like onions- they have layers. All people have layers and we must be aware of this when questioning. For us to find out all that we can in our questioning process we almost take the role of a criminal prosecution lawyer and keep asking questions until beyond all reasonable doubt we can recommend our solutions with confidence.

The technique is to pick a line of questioning and to keep peeling back layers of detail until you have sufficient information, before moving to the next line of questioning.

By following this process, when you then recommend your products and services, you are doing so based on great information.

2 ears and 1 mouth

Some of the best advice I received as a young sales person was the importance of listening. Great questions are great, however if you don't listen to, or benefit from, the answers then you will never take maximum benefit from your opportunities.

Being a great sales professional has nothing to do with having the "gift of the gab" or "having all the answers". Success can be maximised by asking great questions and listening to the responses.

LISTEN is an interesting word as it shares the exact same letters as the word SILENT. Sometimes that's what listening is. Purely by saying nothing at all, your potential customer will continue to share information and much of it will be hugely valuable.

Take time to listen and write notes. By really listening you will hear things that allow you to tailor your recommendations better to their needs, as well as identify countless more opportunities for both now and in the future.

What is this costing you?

My first lesson on pricing was served to me as 14 year old businessman, yet I myself continually find myself making mistake after mistake on pricing.

I meet many business owners who tell me proudly how they convert 100% of their opportunities. The truth is that we should price some of our customers out of the market place and until we do so we have not yet found our optimum price points.

Your price should be calculated by what your product or service is worth to your consumer and not what it costs you. Providing you can provide at a price they are prepared to pay and make a profit, then you are in business.

Toolbox   Maximising opportunities

As your knowledge and experience grows, so does your competence and in turn your prices should follow suit. In every profession experience brings rewards and by improving your sales skills you will be able to better demonstrate your value to your customers and improve your remuneration accordingly.

Test your pricing and continually trial new price points until you are certain that you have found an optimum point. You may then look to introduce a premium and a value offering to sit either side of your core product or service. Around 20% of all your existing customers will buy a premium product if you make it available and around 20% of those who did not buy from you would buy a value offering if that was available too.

The simple upsell

Introducing additional products, at the point of sale, is an incredibly effective way of increasing your customer's average transaction value. Many people feel uncomfortable when introducing an upsell, however let's look at a number of examples where upsells happen every day, and please then decide how you feel about them.

Example 1
Every time you have ever ordered from a leading fast food retailer you will have been invited to "Go large" this simple upsell creates a multi-billion dollar revenue globally each year.

Example 2
Each time you have eaten in a restaurant you will have been invited to order a dessert, after dinner drink or perhaps even both. These incremental sales add as much as 50% to the average transaction value

Example 3
When ordering a coffee from internationally renowned coffee houses you are often encouraged to order larger drinks through the deceptive use of size names. This process can result in an increased spend of up to 20%

Looking at each of those examples I am sure you can picture your own scenarios where these tactics have been used. I would ask you to consider how you feel each time you are up sold to?

In the first 2 examples you are honestly invited to make an increased purchase in relation to your first purchase. You simply provide a yes or no response and your server reacts appropriately. You then enjoy what you have ordered and then move on without much further thought.

The third example leaves a slightly different feeling for me. I feel slightly annoyed if I have been tricked into spending more than I needed to. This is the same feeling I have had when booking low-cost airline tickets and realising the actual price I end up paying is far higher than the advertised price that hooked me into purchasing in the first place.

The lesson I see here is that upsells do work well. To be delivered easily they must be systemised, honest and related to the first person. They must then be offered at every opportunity and then simply act on the customer's response with no further emotion. When offering upsells, some will take you up on your offer and some won't, but the end result of offering them will be a significant increase in sales and little increase in operating costs resulting in substantial additional profits.

Product placement

If you are looking to increase both the frequency of transaction and average order value of your consumers then placing the right products in the right places at the right time can have massive positive impact.

With a background in department store retail this was a key part of our sales success. When designing stores facilities like toilets and restaurants are placed at the back of the stores to ensure customers travel past as much product to reach their destinations. Supermarkets place impulse purchases like magazines and confectionary at the till points to capitalise on the queuing customers and online retailers suggest additional products to you as you fill your online basket.

The successful strategy here comes from linking together useful products and services and then simply putting them in front of your customers.

Product placement works best in 2 key locations.

> 1. At the point of checkout. Whether you have a physical counter, an online checkout or simply send invoices to your customers, the point of payment is an ideal place to introduce simple complimentary purchases.

> 2. In high footfall areas. If you have areas in your business that receive high levels of interest from your existing customers then by placing products in these areas you will crystallise a number of ancillary sales. These areas will include your website homepage, newsletter communications,

meeting rooms and any other areas that your customers utilise extensively.

Multi-buy offers

We become familiar with these offers from the abundance we see in the supermarkets and no doubt have fallen for them ourselves on a number of occasions.

Let's explore what makes them so attractive. What we are talking about here is primarily the "buy one, get one free" and "3 for 2" offers that encourage consumers to buy more than required. As consumers the logic side of our brain kicks in and results in us having to take the offer, as opposed to buying a single item, and will often end in us choosing an alternative brand as a result of the offer.

When retailing ourselves this is a valuable tool, particularly when introducing new products and looking to steer market share away from our competitors. Another great use is when you are looking to sell large quantities of anything and get a lot of product into the market place. Well timed offers, like this, can have a dramatic impact on a market place and create strong exposure very quickly, and result in massive increases in sales.

Membership

Every business has the opportunity of introducing a membership to its customers. I have been involved in creating membership products with car garages, garden centres, hairdressers, online retailers, recruitment companies and many more. I am yet to find an organisation that could not provide a membership solution to its customers.

By introducing membership to your customers, whether through a subscription newsletter, a loyalty scheme or a private members club what you start to do is to create an additional regular revenue stream, as well as keeping your most valuable customers close to you, to encourage additional transactions and referrals.

Asking for referrals

We all know that business referred from an existing customer is our ideal way to win new business, yet still many businesses fail to ask their existing happy customers to introduce them to further customers. Over the years I have developed a simple formula that I use at every given opportunity:

Toolbox   Maximising opportunities

Rule number 1.

If you don't ask you don't get!

Simply asking others for help will result in a better result than not asking at all.

Rule number 2.

There are good times to ask.

For me, there are three times that you can ask for referrals and I would encourage you to ask on each of these occasions:

- When you have just secured an order
- When you have just delivered your product or service
- When you have just successfully handled a complaint or resolved an issue.

Rule number 3.

Know exactly what to say.

Now, you don't have to follow this word for word, but there are some key words that are essential and I have highlighted them in bold.

Maximising opportunities — Toolbox

*You couldn't do me a little **favour**?*

*You wouldn't happen to know **just one person**, who j**ust like you**, would benefit from (insert benefit)?*

Then wait for positive answer!!!

Rule number 4.
Don't take the name and number when first offered. When they first offer the referral, your first action must be to thank them for it, but do not take the contact details. It is essential here that you ask your referral source to contact the referral and gain permission for you to contact, so simply arrange a time for you to call them back for their details once they have agreed you can contact.

Rule number 5.

Make it ok they have not called.

When you make your follow up call open your conversation by saying "I am guessing that you have not got round to calling (insert name)?"

This makes it ok if they have not yet called and they typically do it straight away, or makes them feel great that they have called and then pass you the contact details.

Toolbox Maximising opportunities

You now have a valuable referral that is best positioned to lead to new business.

Data Capture

One of the biggest assets of any business is the value of its database. A key activity to us at all times is to proactively grow our database. We collect full contact details of all customers and look to gain the details of all audiences when we deliver at events and attend shows.

In every interaction when we converse with a customer, or potential customer, we are gathering data that will be useful for future sales and marketing activity. It's really easy to do but equally easy not to do.

If you are looking for people to complete data for you, then please ensure they have the time and resources to do it for you. I often see pubs, hotels and restaurants handing out competition and feedback forms but no pens to complete them!!!

Feedback Forms

Our simple one page feedback forms have been invaluable in growing our business. Take a look and

Maximising opportunities — **Toolbox**

see what information you would like to gather from your customers.

REACHINGNEWHEIGHTS
the route to sales success

Name:

Action points I will implement from today...

1.
2.
3.
4.
5.
6.

Names and numbers of those who have missed out by not being here today:

Would you like to subscribe to the monthly publication ACCELERATOR?
Yes please ☐   No not today ☐

Would you like to purchase an Audio Programme today?
Yes please ☐   No not today ☐

Would you like to discuss how we can help you further with your business?
Yes please ☐   No not today ☐

Positive comment on the day

www.reachingnewheights.co.uk

Be convenient

To this day the best example I have of the power of implementing this lesson is through my current print supplier. I am continually bombarded with the opportunity to change supplier and no doubt my existing supplier is not the cheapest. What they do so well is they make everything really easy for me, they take an order over the phone and give me a 60 day account, they then make minor amends in house to avoid artwork going backwards and forwards and will continually move mountains to meet tight deadlines.

The convenience factor that they provide makes them our default supplier and someone I regularly recommend. Take a look at your own processes and see how easy you make it for your customers. Simply by removing any barriers, and being prepared to be flexible, will win you more business.

Waterproofing

Often once a sale is agreed our immediate focus shifts to continuing on our day, and perhaps even to the next sale. The 24 hour period following a customer making a buying decision is the period where your sale is most vulnerable.

Maximising opportunities — Toolbox

Customers can often suffer from a condition known as "buyer's remorse". This is when they change their mind at a period shortly after confirming their order and look to cancel or amend their order.

If you consider the emotional rollercoaster that people go through during the buying process, there is no surprise that some will have doubts following their initial decision.

The way we prevent this is by having a "what happens next" confirmation. This is so easy to miss but it allows you to set the scene of exactly what they have agreed to and confirms the next actions.

I have often referred to this process as "waterproofing", because what you are doing is preventing any leaks in your order as you depart.

This is a process we used a lot in the furniture industry and a regular scenario would be following the customer selecting their items, the sales staff would provide some care advice that would reiterate the expectation of the performance of furniture and detail what happens next.

Example
"Thank you very much for your order. Your order will be sent off to the factory to you today and components

will be ordered and production space will be booked. Your furniture will then be assembled over the coming weeks and will be delivered to you in around 6 weeks. In the event that the furniture arrives early we will simply call you to arrange a delivery within 48 hours. Are you ok to take delivery early or would you sooner wait? (Await response)

When your furniture arrives it will be professionally installed to the room of your choice and all packaging will be removed. Please remember that your sofas have fibre filled cushions and need to be plumped and turned daily, and the fabric should be vacuumed weekly to extend the life of your furniture. The fabric is to be professionally cleaned so please ensure that you leave that to the experts as opposed to putting it in the washing machine and damaging your furniture.

Any further questions? (Await response) typically no questions, however if there are then simply just answer them.

That's great. Just a quick reminder that your furniture will be ordered today and by confirming this form you are entering into a formal agreement and your order cannot be cancelled at any time. To confirm your order today I just need a quick autograph at the bottom of this simple 1 page form."

By delivering this short presentation we saved countless complaints about delivery times, performance of furniture following delivery and had little to no cancellations following orders. I promise that it is worth the extra time in ensuring all your sales are properly "waterproofed".

Review old diaries and journals

A tool that always brings results for me is to take the time to review my old diaries and journals. I find massive value in running an "old-fashioned" page per day paper diary system. My system has a full page for diary entries and a further page for notes for that day.

This diary travels everywhere with me and is littered with valuable information.

Once a quarter, I go back through my last 3 months diary pages and find actions and ideas that I am still yet to complete, people that I have met with that could now lead to a business opportunity and leads that I failed to contact at the time.

I would go as far to say that my diary system is probably my most valuable asset as a sales professional. It is far more than just a planning tool for meetings and appointments. The notes that I scribble in this are priceless in terms of increased opportunities.

Toolbox   Maximising opportunities

Electronic diaries are great, but typically prevent the creative scribbles that we all make as sales professionals. The scraps of paper, post it notes and single leaves of notepaper we have used to take notes, all get misplaced easily, however a continuous daily journal is so simple yet so valuable if you plan to capitalise on every action that you take and opportunity you create.

Chapter 7
Developing a team

Being individually brilliant is hugely rewarding personally yet having the ability to empower and inspire a team is a complete new level. I have been running sales teams since the age of 18, made countless mistakes and learnt some great tools to get the best out of others. In this chapter you will be introduced to what has worked for me and understand how you can use these lessons in your business. Even if you don't yet have a team you may find the lessons then help you to develop yourself.

The art of sales management

Sales people are often competitive, highly strung, egotistical, outspoken and just south of arrogant. This short list of qualities may just scratch the surface of many sales people and as such they can be notoriously difficult to manage. Control them too much and they will revolt, give them too much rope and they will exploit you.

Mastering this art form really is a massive challenge and as such is regularly overlooked. My experience in this

Developing a team — Toolbox

field means that I would tackle it head on and provide you with the tools that have really helped me.

You never get a second chance to make a first impression

Setting the rules when you take on a new member of sales staff is vital if you want to get the best out of them. Cover everything from company culture and values, to dress code, personal grooming, time keeping, and expectation of performance, but also share with them the consequences of underperformance.

Creatures of Habit

Sales people are creatures of habit. Show them what success looks like and they will follow it. However, please remember that people do two things in business, what they enjoy doing and what they get checked on. As such, my advice is to keep the job fun. Creating a routine that generates activity, but also creates a sense of team and puts a smile on everyone's face, is essential in well managed organisations.

Toolbox   Developing a team

Meeting regularly as a team is important, but consider timing and location wisely. My most successful sales team met every Friday at 3 pm in the pub, for a review of the week, and at 8 am every Tuesday for breakfast to discuss the week ahead. Our results where double that of our competitors.

The challenge can often be that changing a routine is remarkably difficult as sales staff generally don't take well to change. If your existing routine is not working, in terms of results, and does not provide the culture that you are happy with, then it requires strong leadership to change it.

My advice is that if you know that your changes will make a long term improvement, then make an instant decision and stick to it. You will find that sales staff are selling all the time and will start trying to convince you that your changes won't work. Stick to your guns and stay strong. They will soon come round and before long be enjoying the benefits of your changed routine.

Give them a fine reputation to live up to

Great sales people are competitive and although they are often employed by your business, they are typically managed by the most demanding boss in the world – themselves. This information is priceless when motivating your team.

Use questions, when asking more of your team, as opposed to giving orders. Challenging them on the results of others, either past or present, can be very effective. Equally get them to set their own targets, but only when in front of others. The fact that they have publicly shared their goals means that they are far more likely to achieve them.

Use language like
"Rob has sold 4 this week .....I thought that you were better than Rob"

and

"If we started a new sales person next week how many orders should they get in there first 6 weeks? .... So why have you only secured....?"

However please remember that although sales staff may seem thick skinned, they are often emotional and nearly always fragile. As such it is essential that praise is loud, lavish and in public, yet any genuine criticism must happen behind closed doors. Protect their ego, its valuable to you. A sales person lacking confidence and self belief will always under perform.

Toolbox Developing a team

Manage results but measure activity

We are all in business for results yet often the results can be out of our control. With this in mind simply recording the results of your team's efforts can be misleading. I would encourage you to measure not just the outcome from your team's efforts but also the input. This allows you to reward effort, manage complacency and idleness, and most importantly, identify development opportunities.

We have recently started to measure a number of simple KPI's through a sales team with a new client and seen a huge uplift in results.

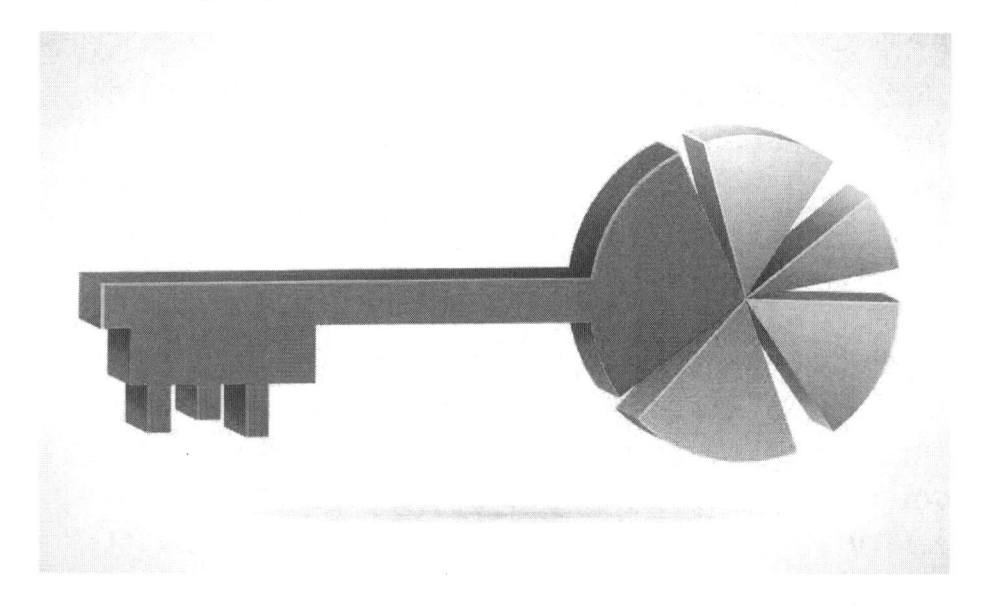

Only once you measure each component of success can you start to manage the overall result by tweaking the success in each area.

Let me show you

As leaders we expect respect yet sometimes we have not quite earned it. I started managing people at the age of 18 and had a substantial barrier to overcome, as I was continually discriminated against because of my age. My rapid promotions through my career have meant that I have always been in bigger roles than my peers, and quite often found myself managing a team of people whose experience in years had surpassed my time on the planet!

Very quickly I learnt that experience really should not be measured in years and people are really judged on what they can do and not what they say they can do. I guess what I really mean is, actions speak louder than words.

As children we learn quickest by seeing what others do, are then impressed or inspired to learn, and then simply observe what they do and keep trying for ourselves until we have mastered it. Using this knowledge I decided that for me to gain the respect of my teams I needed to be able to do things better than they could. I studied books and learnt from those who were performing at high standards. I then practiced and practiced until my competence in all areas made me good enough to teach.

I then took action and started to show people the results of my lessons, as I practiced what I preached, continually outperforming those around me.
Once I had earned their respect I had the ability to impart these skills with massive credibility, I was good enough to teach and was leading by example. When people needed coaching, help and assistance, I could simply show them how to do it and not tell them. What do you do so well and wish others could do as well as you? Let them observe you doing it. Show them everything you do to reach that success and watch your people grow.

Be good enough to teach

Earning the right to teach others comes from having the ability to draw on your own experience and share stories to help others see what they need to do differently.

The best people to train others have been there and done it. They have stood in the shoes of the delegate and have countless scenarios they can impart on others.

All too often training is seen as a luxury and not delivered effectively. Your team is only as good as the people in it and ongoing training is essential to keep them performing at their best. If you consider the world's best sports teams, they are full of talented individuals, and continue to train every day remaining focussed on their prize.

The best trainers have all got experience of knowing exactly what it takes to excel in a role. Yes you can learn to be a trainer but you can only gain real life experience by living it.

For this reason many teams don't get trained on sales skills at all. They are trained on product knowledge and company processes but the skills to win new business are reliant on existing experience and luck.

Imagine your favourite football club recruiting the best footballer in the world and relying on them to just bring their existing skills and experience. Anyone who stops learning is going backwards.

If you want the best from your team every day, then their continuous professional development from specialists is essential. It amazes me that all the people

Toolbox   Developing a team

I have ever trained always leave having been reminded of something they already knew, as well as learning new skills. Bad habits and complacency are costing businesses a fortune and staying sharp, continuing to grow, could make a massive difference.

Chapter 8
Dealing with indecision

I am sure at some stage you have had a customer remain undecided after your sales presentation, and after all your hard work provides you with an objection, excuse or reason why they cant do business at this time. I have done huge amounts of work in this area and of all the objections I have ever heard they typically fall into one of the following examples.

- Not the right time
- Need to discuss with someone else
- Awaiting other quotes
- Happy with existing supplier
- Need some time to think about it
- Too expensive

Avoiding objections

Pretty much every objection that you have ever faced will have been avoidable by asking great questions

Dealing with indecision — Toolbox

earlier on in the sales process. Take a look at your most common objections and have a think about how they can be avoided before you ever even recommend your solution. Consider that most objections are purely excuses and preventing them from using that excuse will dramatically increase your conversion rates.

When selling furniture we faced several objections and one of the items that we were measured on was the number of sales that we could encourage customers to order a footstool in addition to their order.

Our most common objection was that the customer did not have room for a footstool.

Knowing this was the typical objection we would face we learned to ask questions early on in the sales discussion that prevented the customer giving this excuse later on. Quite simply, if I could get them to admit they could use an extra seat, enjoyed putting their feet up and had a decent size room it became remarkably difficult to not include a footstool in their order.

We developed questions such as

"*Apart from yourself who will be using the furniture?*" and then follow with the question "*And a spot of entertaining?*" After getting the initial users everybody

Toolbox   Dealing with indecision

would admit to entertaining. I guess nobody admits to having no friends?

This would equip me with the knowledge that they will have more people using the furniture than they currently have seats.

I would then ask.

"*What room is it going in?*" regardless of the answer I would then ask "I*s that the best room or the everyday room?*" regardless of the answer I would then ask "*What size is the room?*" and regardless of the answer I would respond with the statement "*Oh, that's a fair size room.*"

At that point I would be pretty certain that they could benefit from a footstool and would have the space for it. If I was in any doubt I would ask them to draw the room complete with new furniture and focal points. I would then always find room for a footstool.

Taking this time to truly qualify a customer before presenting solutions is the key skill in avoiding objections and increasing success. My definition of professional salesmanship is that

> "*Selling is earning the right to make a recommendation*"

Dealing with indecision Toolbox

Without earning the right you are simply guessing and guessing will always bring mixed results.

Magic words – I bet you are a bit like me...?

Getting people to agree with you is a very valuable tool in salesmanship and simple sequences of words that can get customers to do exactly that can be priceless.

I learnt that if I could paint a picture of me taking a reasonable action and then ask others to agree with me, it became rapid fire way of getting people to agree quickly.

The words I would use to pre-face any statement are the words "I bet you are a bit like me?" and subtly nod whilst saying it.

Examples include

"I bet you are bit like me and enjoy nothing more than getting home from work, grabbing a drink and putting your feet up in front of the TV?"

"I bet you are bit like me and always learn loads from reading books but always need some help to take further action?"

Toolbox — Dealing with indecision

"I bet you are a bit like me and have not yet got round to making sufficient plans for your retirement?"

Overcoming Objections

Every objection really should be treated as a disagreement, and you should take personal responsibility that they have raised an objection, as it may mean that they have grabbed the wrong end of the stick. Throughout the years I have developed a simple system that acts as a framework to overcome every objection presented to you.

> **1. Clarify objection** - Remember that success in sales is all about maintaining control of the process. The second they raise an objection they are challenging that control and can easily switch it. Think about an interview scenario, it's the person asking the questions that is in complete control. Knowing this, if we treat every objection as a question and look to regain control by asking a further question we get closer to the real objection. Ideal questions are simply getting them to explain their objection further and my default response is simply "What makes you say that?"
>
> **2. Agree/Apologise** – Given that we are viewing this as a disagreement we can easily deflate it and

find some level ground by agreeing with them and then apologising. Once we have done this we have a platform to respond from and don't fight fire with fire.

If someone objected because they needed to speak to their business partner first I would say something like.

"I am really sorry to put you in this awkward position. I would not make important decisions without consulting with others first."

3. Check if it the only concern – By asking if this is the only factor stopping them from moving forward, if they agree, you have only one objection to overcome. Missing this step can result in a game of tennis as further objections are continually presented as each is overcome.

4. Receive it positively – Take the fact that they have objected as that they are interested in what you do and not that they are not interested. It will have a very positive impact on your posture.

5. Answer positively – It is very easy to focus on what you cannot do when somebody presents you with an objection. Simply focus on what you can do instead. If the objection was based on price, then simply explain what you can do for their budget instead.

6. Summary close – After explaining what you can do the safest closing tool when dealing with indecision is to close in summary form. Simply break the decision into between 5 and 10 small decisions and ask direct "yes" focussed questions, knowing that when they say "yes" to each question they then agree to the whole thing.

Magic words –
Just out of curiosity

Our role as sales people is to give our customers enough information to make a decision and then invite them to take the next step. When customers are stuck in the land of indecision, we have to make some direct statements or ask some direct questions to get them off the fence and help them make their mind up. This is difficult to do and, for fear of appearing rude, we choose not to ask and step away from the opportunity.

To soften these direct approaches, I have developed a simple sequence of words that makes asking a lot easier. Simply by prefacing your questions with the words "Just out of curiosity…" you will instantly feel more comfortable when making strong points- without appearing confrontational.

Examples would be:

> *"Just out of curiosity, what needs to happen for you to commit to this?"*

> *"Just out of curiosity, what is stopping you?"*

> *"Just out of curiosity, what exactly is it specifically that you would like to think about?"*

Prefacing with these words will drastically improve your results, because you will ask things that you would have otherwise avoided.

Negotiate like a pro

Business is simple but not easy. The difference between average and great is typically the last 10% of the process, and can quite often be the time when most people give up. The ability to negotiate effectively when you do not get your own way will make a significant contribution to your success and be infinitely more rewarding. To help I will share 9 simple tips to help you become a master negotiator and ensure that people come round to your way of thinking more often.

Arguments end with losers – Nobody wants to be a loser and the problem with arguing in a sales environment is that if you are the winner then your prospect is the loser. Avoid arguments at all costs.

Show Respect for the other person's opinions – Now you don't have to agree with them but they are entitled to their opinion. Understand their reasons for their point of view and look to understand.

Admit when you are wrong – Admitting to what you don't know or have got wrong will add weight to anything that you do know.

Encourage the easy Yes – To bring prospects around to your point of view ask multiple simple questions that lead to "Yes" answers. By doing so, your prospect will find it easier to continue saying yes.

Talk Less – The biggest reason for a misunderstanding or failure to communicate effectively is not listening.

Let the other person believe that it is their idea -Introduce your ideas as questions and not statements. That way, your prospect can choose your point of view as their own.

Try honestly to see thing from the other person's point of view - This may seem hard however it is vital to show empathy when negotiating. Put yourself in their shoes and it will help you understand why they think what they think. This angle will add substance to your side of the negotiation.

Dramatise your ideas - Whether selling a product, service or an idea, enthusiasm always helps to convince. Simply by becoming more charismatic when presenting your viewpoint you will make it far easier to agree with your line of thinking.

Throw down a challenge – In conclusion always finish your negotiations with a challenge or ultimatum. A good example would be "*So if I can get this done today are we okay to confirm the order now?*"

However, expert negotiation comes with practice. To practice at first, you must not give up too easily, and believe in yourself. Typically it is mix of skill and confidence that wins a negotiation.

Toolbox   Dealing with indecision

The Big Negotiation

Me and my big mouth can often get me into trouble and I once found myself in an incredibly challenging negotiation that went on to teach me a fantastic lesson and provide me with a fantastic tool.

I was working in my property business and had a disagreement with my partner on the deal he had presented me to sell on a new resort. It was our biggest ever project and the challenge was that the prices we needed to sell at to secure our margins resulting in me and my team having a very difficult job to do. I therefore challenged my colleague and suggested that he could have got a better deal and before long found myself on the way to Cyprus. Given that I felt so strongly that a better deal could be negotiated, I had been volunteered to arrange a meeting and negotiate a better price.

When I arrived I was presented with a glamorous boardroom full of smoke and six representatives of the developer there to meet with me. Three I knew well and three were completely new to me.

It was a challenging discussion, but throughout I believed that we were the only people that could help them to sell the properties and that I needed the right prices to give great value to my customers. As the debate unfolded, they would break out into conversations in Greek, before coming back in English and after 2 hours of negotiation they came back to me with the question, "Is that your best offer?"

I paused and with confidence simply replied "Yes" and sat back in my chair and remained silent for what seemed like an eternity. Just as the sweat started to bead on my forehead, George said "Is this one of those situations when the next person who speaks loses?" I then just smiled and pushed the contract across the table.

The contract was promptly signed and we secured the deal we needed.

The lesson it served was the power of a pause- less is more and confidence is king!

Magic Words – Don't Worry

In sales and negotiations it is important that we diffuse the situation as quick as we possibly can. Two words that can quickly bring calm to a difficult situation are the words "Don't Worry". They can instantly bring reassurance and turn big challenges into smaller ones. The fact that you use these words and remain calm and

Toolbox   Dealing with indecision

controlled in your tone brings comfort to your customer or prospect. These words can be used at the beginning of a customer call, when talking about a difficult situation, and when a customer is in indecision and has worries about taking the next step and agreeing an order.

Examples would be:

- Don't worry you are speaking to exactly the right person
- Don't worry we have seen this situation many times before and are perfectly equipped to help
- Don't worry I understand your current point of view and I am sorry that is how you currently feel...
- Don't worry you are bound to feel nervous and that's exactly why we are here to help you

Can I have a discount?

Regardless of the level of experience in business we have all been asked for discounts and most of us have asked for discounts ourselves. When challenged for a discount ourselves, we all too often buckle and end up providing our products and services for less than they are worth. Consider a scenario where

Dealing with indecision — Toolbox

perhaps you have asked for a discount in your life, perhaps a substantial purchase like a house or a car.

When you achieved a reduction in price I would imagine you felt a sense of achievement and satisfaction ... Only later to ask yourself the question wondering whether they would have gone any lower. In the same scenario the seller is equally questioning whether you would have paid more and the end result is that both parties are not convinced they achieved the best deal.

When we buy something in a high street chain, we just accept the price is the price and are happy we got the best deal and I believe that we can learn from these scenarios.

My advice is simple. Ensure that your price represents great value for money and protect it at all costs.
So when challenged on price then you are actually entering a negotiation and in all successful negotiations I look for two winners and not a winner and a loser. With this in mind it is about give and take. If you are being asked for a better price then think; what can you take in return? Things to consider are as follows.

- Increased order size
- Long term commitment from the customer
- Improved payment terms
- Introduction to another organisation you can do business with

Toolbox   **Dealing with indecision**

However what people are asking for in a discount is the best deal possible. To identify how you can help design the best deal, the first action to take when challenged on price is to respond to their request for a discount with a question.

The question I would use would be …. "Just out of curiosity……..Why would you like a discount?" said with a big smile.

The response to this question will then help you design an offer that best suits their needs without giving a discount. Things to consider are as follows:

- Increased payment terms.
- Giving extra instead of reducing price
- If their budget does not stretch then reducing specification

The conditional close

I am sure in the past you have been asked to move from your standard pricing, terms and conditions or timescales from a customer. Whenever a customer asks us to move from standard terms before considering your move you should regain control with a conditional close.

Dealing with indecision — Toolbox

Quite simply a conditional is "If I can …… Will you ……?"

Examples include

> *"If I can secure that price will you be ordering today?"*
>
> *"If I can meet your delivery deadlines will you pay today?"*
>
> *"If I can change those terms for you will you commit to us as an exclusive supplier?"*

Shifting the control back in this way means that you only have to give something away in return for an action from them and can help bring scenarios to decision quickly.

Be persistent

We all have dream customers and will have made several approaches for great opportunities that have not resulted in success. We take lack of success in sales very personally and feel bruised by our failure, often taking this rejection as a forever decision – never to re-visit again.

Toolbox   Dealing with indecision

As consumers our circumstances are changing all the time and the same is true with our customers. Whatever is considered 'the wrong time' for our potential customers, it could change to the right time as soon as the day after. Once we understand this, it is paramount that we keep ourselves in the minds of our customers and never ever forget a prospect.

I keep a list of all my NNT's (No not today's) and continue to stay in touch, ensuring that I am the first person they think of when their circumstances change.

This includes communicating with them in the following ways.

- Regular emails or newsletters
- Adding them to your social networks
- Popping in to say "Hello"
- Picking up the phone

Let's focus on the point of just picking up the phone. It continually amazes me what can be achieved by simply picking up the phone and speaking to the people you wish to do business with.

A short while ago I was looking for a very successful business personality called Dr Joanna Martin to complete an article for my Accelerator publication.

Dealing with indecision · Toolbox

I secured the article, without fee, by simply picking up the phone and asking for it!

A good friend and mentor of mine tells a great story of persistence and how it helped land the largest training contract he had ever secured, which has supported him and his family with a fabulous lifestyle. He called his dream customer every week at the same time for 18 months and continually got no further than the personal assistant. However, not put off from achieving his goal he continued to call, and after building great rapport with the PA finally got put through to the owner and won his appointment.

This resulted in revolutionising his business and without question was well worth the effort. My advice is to never, ever, ever, ever give up!

Playing Devil's Advocate

During my time in the property business we developed a fantastic long term investment product where the model involved owning a freehold property in the sun that you could use personally and would turn an initial investment of £20,000 into a £200,000 lump sum over a period of years and then continue to produce an income.

Toolbox — Dealing with indecision

Everybody that I spoke with about this opportunity loved the idea and would ask if I could send them an email or leave them a brochure. I soon learnt that neither of these options resulted in success and knew that something needed to change.

The true challenge was that I could not get enough potential customers to the point that they had anything they could make a decision upon and at best I would gain a conceptual interest.

I started to think about the times that me, my brothers and sister had sat as children and entered into the land of make believe with the Argos catalogue and happily made decisions about items that we would like to buy, but purely in a hypothetical sense. It was this peculiar logic that lead me to develop a closing technique that I have since named the "Devils advocate" close.

Each time I established a level of interest from a potential customer that fitted my target market I would simply pre face my qualifying questions with the words.

"Let's just play devil's advocate for a second..."

I would then take them through a series of questions that would result in the fact that if they were to invest in a freehold property then it would be a specific one within a specific resort.

Once you can get to this point you can then show them exactly what they need to consider to make a buying decision and finish by finding out what is stopping them from moving forward today.

This simple process resulted in securing orders from 32% of the customers that would have otherwise just asked me to leave it with them. That's not a bad return in my book!

Chapter 9
Account Management

Managing existing customers is a huge part of big businesses and they often have entire departments for this function alone. The fundamental understanding is that in the role of account management the sole purpose is to retain customers and therefore you must continually remind them to buy from you. In today's fast-paced world, no one tool is sufficient. We must consider multiple forms of communication if we are to get the most from our customer relationships. We use an ever expanding number of tools and have made mistakes and gained best practice from each of them.

The Database

Without question a good database is the hub of all great account management processes. A database should include all relevant contact details for all customers, suppliers and potential customers. It should show their past value to you financially, and also include their expected future value. You should then keep an up to date biography on each person in your database allowing others to understand your relationship, and it should store any useful facts. Attached to each record you should then keep a running timeline of contact and correspondence, allowing you to always have great information to recall. In addition the ability to forward plan and set reminders prevent you from needing a perfect memory.

Years ago systems that provided this service were a significant investment and small businesses relied on spread sheets, diaries and client files. Technological advances mean that you can access software that provides a framework to do all of this, at no further expense to yourself. Simply enter the phrase "business CRM system" into your search engine and you will be impressed with incredible choice.

The Drop in

Without question the most effective way to remind your customers to shop with you is by simply dropping in face to face. Sometimes un-announced, perhaps arranged at short notice or even a scheduled meeting; every time you meet with a potential customer, you will have the opportunity to further cement your relationship and uncover new areas that you can help each other.

The Courtesy call

We have already established that picking up the phone is a catalyst for making stuff happen. Please don't forget your existing customers and schedule regular calls to discuss the account. This is your chance to check that they are happy with the work completed to date, as well as gain insight into their future plans, and what you can do to assist.

The Newsletter

Sending a regular hard copy newsletter to your existing customers can become a fantastic way of keeping them engaged with your business and ensuring that you are kept in mind. The question of how often you write a newsletter will continue to go unanswered. My take is that you should be consistent with its frequency and write as often as you have something worth saying. Being paper based it should be simple to read and full of images. Consider that it will be read as a break from the daily routine, so this should ideally be light entertainment.

The E-newsletter

The biggest difference between your electronic newsletter and its paper based rival is that only the minority of people you send it to will actually open it, let alone read it. Therefore it must be concise and to the point. Look to deliver value to your subscribers and consider what simple pieces of advice you can give them that they can act on quickly and easily. The more value you give the more impact these will have.

The Blog

This is a fantastic tool to position yourself as an expert within your industry. Ideally attached to your website you can regularly post your thoughts, ideas and opinions on matters that will be of interest to your communication. Having a blog gives you a voice to share great information. Simply by having a blog and writing about your area of knowledge will result as you being seen as an authority within your market place.

The Facebook page

Soon to become an essential tool for every business, having a presence on facebook is really a chance for you to connect with your customers on a social level. Imagine with your facebook page you are hosting a dinner party for all your members and you should entertain them accordingly. Be courteous when they arrive and show interest in them. Post content that they personally will be interested in and don't just broadcast customer offers.

If you choose to use facebook as a tool, then please learn from the big companies and do all you can to build your audience on your page. Ensure that your account is easy to find and promote it through all of your other marketing activities. One of the best run small business pages is owned by a lady that I had the pleasure of sharing a stage with in Northampton in 2011. The lady in question is Hannah Macleod who owns a company called Coulson Macleod. Check out their page and you will see what I mean.

The Twitter account

Imagine twitter like the busiest ever train station in rush hour. Conversations are happening everywhere and you are not sure what to say or who to listen to, but know doubt there will be a few interesting conversations going on.

I find twitter far more useful listening to others and joining conversations, rather than looking for something profound to say myself. Follow all of your key customers and pay attention to what they are posting. Re-tweet their posts and join in their discussions if you want them to notice you.

Educating customers on the use of the # symbol when grouping information can allow them to communicate in groups effectively and easily. We used #toolboxtour throughout our one day events launching this book and can then easily track all comments related to our events and respond accordingly.

The Linkedin account

Connecting with all your existing customers on Linkedin can give you huge benefits. Firstly, you can learn so much more about them from their detailed personal profile, but also you have gained a further way of directly contacting them. A Linkedin email can often generate a higher open rate than standard emails and get you noticed more effectively.

A further benefit is, that if your contact ever moves on career wise, you are connecting to them as an individual and not via the business. That way it will be easy to contact them again once they reach their new role

A further tool with Linkedin is to create groups. By creating a group for your customers you again have a further method of communication and can create a community for your customers and add huge value to them.

The Website

Your website is a fantastic tool to manage your existing customers. Every time you bring people to your website you have the chance to introduce additional products and services to them.

If you provide resources to your customers then make them available from your website and introduce additional offers and products to them on their journey to reach their resource.

Your social media and email campaigns will all drive traffic back to your site and well positioned offers will bring results.

Account Management | Toolbox

The Get together

The big corporates know the value of getting their best customers together for high level hospitality scenarios. Getting your customers together and demonstrating how you value them is a proven method of increasing their loyalty. You do not need to invest huge sums to get the same results though. We have used new product launches, low priced events, celebrations and office moves all as excuses to get our customers together and have always gained positive results. We now look to receive added value from these events by encouraging our existing customers to bring guests and we very often find ourselves soon to be doing business with the guests to.

The Letter

Keeping things simple, let's just focus on the letters you already send your customers- perhaps statements, reminders or even invoices. Each of these letters provides a sales opportunity and every form of outbound communication can carry an additional message as well a primary purpose.

Consider the extra value you can get from every mailing by adding a small message or including a

| Toolbox | Account Management |

secondary communication. This is another example of making your own luck.

The Email offer

Many of us receive far too many emails and sales emails become very easy to ignore. They are very useful to broadcast a great offer quickly and at modest cost however our experience is that this method is increasingly losing effectiveness.

To gain good results you must first ensure that each campaign is correctly targeted, as opposed to sending the same message to all you can. Once targeted you really have a number of barriers to overcome.

Barrier number 1 Getting your offer opened.
Just getting an email opened can be challenging and relies purely on a compelling headline. Just like newspapers, the better the headline the better the uptake. Your headline should be designed simply to get the email opened and not to sell your product. The best emotion to trigger, to ensure successful open rates, is intrigue. By leaving the recipient intrigued as to the purpose of the email the only way they can find out is by opening it.
We collect emails that are sent to us, that have

resulted in us opening them and continually learn from headlines used by others. Remember that success leaves clues.

Barrier number 2 Getting your offer read.
Once your mail is opened a reflex decision will be made as to whether to read it or not. Your opening sentence must capture the reader and encourage them to read more. Sub-headlines can help to lead people through the copy and make reading it more simple.

Barrier number 3 Getting them to take action
If your offer gets read it is paramount that the call to action is clear, prominent and repeated. It should be as simple as possible for your reader to take action and painted out in clear simple steps. Confusion at this stage will result in no action taken and no sale. By repeating your action 2 – 3 times throughout your offer you can increase your click through rates by as much as 25%. A simple area to reiterate your call to action is by using a P.S.

Toolbox   Account Management

The Direct mail offer

With email communication becoming less effective for us we are starting to revert back to the traditional methods that have served us so well for years. Using ink on paper to communicate with customers will never go out of fashion.

With the world leaning primarily towards digital communications, we are receiving less and less post through our door, and it is very rare that we receive anything personally addressed that is not a bill. We have always sent hand written cards as a valuable tool and have now taken this further by looking at low volume targeted direct mail campaigns. In a recent test we measured the inbound enquiry level from a very simple split test direct mailing.

We produced a flyer offer to be sent to just 100 existing customers. 50 were sent on their own, with a generic covering letter which resulted in just 4 enquiries. For the other 50 we wrote a very short personal message on a post-it note and adhered it to each flyer before sending. This resulted in an enquiry rate of 21 from 50, an improvement of over 400%

Account Management · Toolbox

The Gift

Corporate gifts have been around for years and the gift market is a huge industry. Yet still I see mistake after mistake as, with the best intention, companies provide gifts that are of little value to their customers and in turn provide little return on investment.

Diaries, calendars, mouse mats, mobile phone holders, cheap pens and stress balls are all examples of gifts I have received that have all passed over my desk without a second thought.

We can all think of elaborate gifts we can use that will increase our value to our customers, but with a little thought there are some great cost effective solutions too.

In 2010 new were sourcing a simple gift to say thank you to our existing customers and we had a very limited budget. I thought about the things that I use that are important to me and that each of my customers could find use for. I then wanted something that would be received with high perceived value and then go on to actually be used for a fair length of time. We settled on producing a high quality personalised notebook subtly detailing our company logo and sharing some useful tips inside. The gifts were very well received however it was 13 months later before I saw their true value.

Toolbox   Account Management

One of the books was gifted to a customer called Paul 'Sound Guy' Spicer who owns a fantastic Audio Visual company that arranges sound and light for a number of high profile events.

For a while we had been in communication with a large national business exhibitions company about me speaking at their events and were getting nothing but standard polite responses.

Paul was then arranging the sound for one of their events and was liaising with their events manager to plan the set up. Paul was taking notes of her ideas and drawing a plan of the room set up. The book he wrote his notes in was the book I gifted him over a year prior.

The events manager noticed my logo, quizzed Paul on my ability and his experience of working with me and Paul gave a glowing response. Within the hour our office phone rang and I was booked to speak at four events.

The Pat on the back

All business leaders and decision makers love recognition. Whether a simple thank you, or some lavish praise, providing it is delivered with sincerity it is a great way of adding value to your customers.

Account Management

Saying thank you is a minimum, but let me share some of the tools that we use to further enhance our customer relationships.

Seeing the little things – I will often look with interest to find ways of congratulating my customers on making a significant achievement. Perhaps receiving an industry standard or being featured in the press would be a great reason to send a card or message. It is paramount that you look at the things that are important to them.

I recently noticed that the daughter of a customer of mine was in the local paper for winning a swimming tournament. Being a parent myself I knew how proud he would have been of this achievement, so I sent him a simple handwritten note in a card. Upon receipt he called to thank me for the card and during the discussion agreed some further work we can do together.

Certificates - For all our training programmes we recognise those who attend by providing them with framed certificates. Not only do they make the recipient feel a little better to have been recognised, but many of these certificates get displayed in offices and act as further referral generation tools.

Toolbox Account Management

Awards – We use our large open events as the opportunity to celebrate success of our best customers. We provide a high quality glass award to recognise sales excellence in our customers.

The text message

This is the only method of communication that you can guarantee will always get read. The world can stop for a text message as people stop mid conversation to check their phones.

The text message should be used as a timely reminder for simple actions. One of the best uses I see, is when fast food delivery retailers send their latest offers by text to previous customers on Friday afternoons.

They all tune into the same station

In every communication with a customer it is important that you understand that really only tune into one frequency. The station they are listening to is called Wii FM and stands for "what's in it for me?"

With every statement you make you must put yourself in the customer's shoes and ask yourself "So what?" in doing so you will ensure that all your communication is benefit lead.

It is the thought that counts

When you take a retrospective look at your life and reflect on the recognition, praise and rewards showered upon you I am certain you are able to count on one hand the number of occasions you remember vividly and which have really left their mark.

As a final thought I want you to consider acknowledging those of value to you and your business. In today's fast paced society, taking time to recognise effort above and beyond the call of duty will give your business the edge and make you leap out from the crowd. Whether you wish to reward excellence in your team, show gratitude to a valued customer, celebrate success with an introducer or influence a prospect, showing your appreciation will bring significant returns.

Financial reward can be an incentive but rarely the best option and over time could cost a fortune. You've heard it said that 'it's the thought that counts' and in business this gives us a chance to shine. Rain genuine praise on your employees when they achieve, say thank you to your customers at every given opportunity, let your introducers know their efforts are appreciated and do all you can to go the extra mile.

Those of you that know me will be aware of the positive feedback I've received using hand written cards. With email overload and the whole world going mobile, a successful way of getting noticed is to go back to basics. Sending a hand written card or letter in acknowledgment of achievements or just to say thank you will win you respect and appreciation. I believe it is possible to build a business by sending cards to customers and prospects, as there are so many opportunities to say thank you or acknowledge special occasions. The sincerity of the message is all important.

It should be personal and heartfelt, don't use the occasion to send marketing literature. Take the time to write neatly by hand and also consider the timing. If you want different results and to be seen as different from your competitors, then start behaving differently.

With special thanks to

Chris Williams

Mark Tonks

Peter Lee

Lorna Sheldon

Dr Joanna Martin

Peter Thomson

Richard Denny

Nan Jones

Jim Rohn

About the author

Since the age of 14, Phil has been practising, developing and fine tuning his sales process. His vast experience in a variety of sectors has resulted in him being recognised as an authority of sales psychology and negotiation, for increasing corporate turnover and profitability, and business development.

With a track record of progressing processes for organisations at all levels, Phil is acknowledged for his strategic intellect and has been instrumental in turning around underperforming businesses by surfacing new opportunities.

Phil, a regular guest speaker, has worked with organisations such as Debenhams and DFS furniture as well as professional football clubs including Birmingham City and Leicester City. In addition he has a wealth of experience in the business sector, which includes evolving a large investment property business, before launching his portfolio of training businesses.

Using the lessons that are taught within the Reaching New Heights one day workshop, Phil and his reliable

About the Author — Toolbox

team have helped thousands of business owners and sales professionals to develop new skills and maximise their potential. Through his speaking, coaching and writing, he has achieved an enviable reputation for developing successful tailored sales processes and achieving peak performance from sales teams; and has also won a number of awards for his work.

Due to the high levels of success, Phil decided to share this opportunity with other like-minded business professionals by launching the Reaching New Heights network of business mentors, with a team delivering the lessons of the workshop and coaching business owners across the globe.

Put simply; Phil has accomplished more than most in his fast-moving life. He has developed processes and procedures which help people to win more customers, who are encouraged to invest more frequently and return more often. Phil is not a theorist, but is a business educator who gives straight talking advice learned from his own experience.

Toolbox   About the Author

Books that have changed my life

How to Win Friends and Influence People - Dale Carnegie

Selling to Win - Richard Denny

The Slight Edge - Jeff Olsen (audio)

Questions are the Answers - Allan Pease

Sales Bible - Jeffrey Gitomer

The Richest Man in Babylon - George S Clayson

Think and Grow Rich - Napoleon Hill

Fish! - Stephen C Lundin

The Success Principles - Jack Canfield (audio)

Who moved my Cheese? - Spencer Johnson

Screw it lets do it! - Richard Branson

The tipping point - Malcolm Gladwell

For further information on Phil Jones or to see how he could help you in your business, please contact

philmjones
helping your business reach new heights

0808 1080 163
enquiries@philmjones.com
Visit www.philmjones.com

Notes...